BOOKISHNESS

LITERATURE NOW

LITERATURE NOW

MATTHEW HART, DAVID JAMES, AND
REBECCA L. WALKOWITZ, SERIES EDITORS

Literature Now offers a distinct vision of late-twentieth- and early-twenty-
first-century literary culture. Addressing contemporary literature and the
ways we understand its meaning, the series includes books that are comparative and transnational in scope as well as those that focus on national
and regional literary cultures.

For a complete list of titles, see page 197

BOOKISHNESS

LOVING BOOKS IN
A DIGITAL AGE

JESSICA PRESSMAN

Columbia University Press   *New York*

Columbia University Press
Publishers Since 1893
New York   Chichester, West Sussex
cup.columbia.edu
Copyright © 2020 Columbia University Press

Library of Congress Cataloging-in-Publication Data
Names: Pressman, Jessica, author.
Title: Bookishness : loving books in a digital age / Jessica Pressman.
Description: New York : Columbia University Press, [2020] |
Series: Literature now | Includes bibliographical references and index.
Identifiers: LCCN 2020022437 (print) | LCCN 2020022438 (ebook) |
ISBN 9780231195126 (hardcover) | ISBN 9780231195133 (trade paperback) |
ISBN 9780231551199 (ebook)
Subjects: LCSH: Books—Social aspects. | Books and reading—
Social aspects. | Literature and technology.
Classification: LCC Z116.A2 P87 2020 (print) | LCC Z116.A2 (ebook) |
DDC 302.23/2—dc23
LC record available at https://lccn.loc.gov/2020022437
LC ebook record available at https://lccn.loc.gov/2020022438

Columbia University Press books are printed on permanent
and durable acid-free paper.
Printed in the United States of America

Cover design: Noah Arlow

To Jonah and Sydney

CONTENTS

List of Illustrations ix

Acknowledgments xi

Introduction 1

1 How and Now Bookishness 25

2 Shelter 41

3 Thing 61

4 Fake 85

5 Weapon 109

6 Memorial 129

Coda 149

Notes 157

Index 185

ILLUSTRATIONS

Figure 0.1 Twelve South's BookBook for iPhone 2

Figure 0.2 Headboard made from books 3

Figure 0.3 Necklace comprising miniature books 4

Figure 0.4 Store window in New Orleans using books as decorations 5

Figure 0.5 Bookish cupcakes by Cakes and Cupcakes Mumbai 6

Figure 0.6 Twelve South's Mac BookBook 7

Figure 0.7 Pamela Paulsrud's *Touchstones* (2013) 9

Figure 0.8 Brian Dettmer, *New Funk Standards* (2017) 9

Figure 0.9 Jane Austen duvet cover 11

Figure 1.1 Apple iBook app interface 36

Figure 3.1 Three-dimensional text in Amaranth Borsuk and Brad Bouse's *Between Page and Screen* (2012) 70

Figure 3.2 Final shot of *The Joy of Books* (2012) 75

Figure 3.3 Page layout from Leanne Shapton's *Important Artifacts and Personal Property from the Collection of Lenore Doolan and Harold Morris, Including Books, Street Fashion, and Jewelry* (2009) 81

Figure 4.1 Example of a "blook" 90

Figure 4.2 Stack of books as home décor, from Target.com 91

Figure 4.3 Bookish comforter that you can read while resting in bed 92

Figure 4.4 *Pride and Prejudice* leggings 93

Figure 4.5 Slipcover and bookish insert elements in J. J. Abrams and Doug Dorst's *S.* (2013) 98

Figure 4.6 Fake marginalia in the pages of J. J. Abrams and Doug Dorst's *S.* (2013) 99

Figure 4.7 Screenshot from the augmented-reality narrative game *The Ice-Bound Concordance* (2016) 104

Figure 4.8 Bookishness in *The Ice-Bound Compendium* 106

Figure 5.1 Excerpt from *House of Leaves*, the remastered, full-color edition, by Mark Z. Danielewski (2000) 113

Figure 5.2 Concrete poetry shark in Steven Hall's *The Raw Shark Texts* (2007) 122

Figure 5.3 Flipbook sequence of shark emerging from depths 123

Figure 6.1 Page layout from Jonathan Safran Foer's die-cut book *Tree of Codes* (2010) 130

Figure 6.2 Front cover of Jonathan Safran Foer's *Tree of Codes* 132

Figure 6.3 Doug Beube bookwork sculpture, *Inside Macintosh* (2005) 144

Figure C.1 Paper email 154

ACKNOWLEDGMENTS

This is a book about feeling attached—to books, bookish identities and communities, and more—and this book only came into the world because of my personal attachments over the last decade. After such a long, nonlinear path, it is a privilege to be able to thank those who supported me along the way.

I was eight months pregnant (and had to get permission from my doctor to travel), but I flew from New Haven, Connecticut, to Ann Arbor, Michigan, to speak at the Bookishness symposium that Jonathan Freedman organized at the University of Michigan.

Jonathan Freedman took a chance on me, a very green professor. He invited me to participate alongside two of the scholars I most respected, Alan Liu and Leah Price, and then published my talk in the *Michigan Quarterly Review* (after great editorial insights, for which I remain grateful). Jonathan Freedman is one of the more generous scholars I know, and I thank him for that first push that helped produce this book.

The bookishness article in the fall 2009 issue of *Michigan Quarterly Review* remained the only thing published from this book for a long while, but it was enough. The topic had legs, and it gave me passage to explore the idea of bookishness through a series of talks given at beautiful universities and with brilliant audiences. These include the Yale Beinecke History of the Book lecture series, the University of Utrecht (The Netherlands), Amsterdam University (The Netherlands), Justus-Liebig-Universität (Germany), Konstanz University (Germany), Michigan State University, NYU Abu Dhabi, UCLA, UCSB, USC, University of Iowa, SDSU, the Shota Rustaveli Institute of Georgian Literature (Tbilisi, Georgia), and the University of Southern Denmark. I am grateful to Kiene Brillenburg Wurth, Heike Schaeffer, Anna Weigel, Justus Nieland, Tom August, Erin Graff Zivin, Irma Ratiani, Rita Felski, and others for invitations to share my work. I am also deeply in debt to the generous and insightful interlocutors who asked questions, offered critiques, sent follow-up suggestions, and otherwise helped shape this book.

This book was also written over a period of personal and professional ambulation. I left a tenure-track job at Yale to move with my family (and to my extended family) to my hometown of San Diego. I arrived with no job prospects, but friends quickly emerged. UCSD offered safe landing under the generous guidance of Michael Davidson. I found a space to lecture about books in the digital age and an invaluable friendship with Liz Losh. Stefan Tanaka gave me freedom to spread my wings by organizing a digital humanities lecture series and a platform from which to build a professional life in my hometown. Seth Lerer kept me feeling scholarly, and Lev Manovich reminded me why I love the digital arts. Joanna Brooks found me at UCSD and stewarded me to SDSU. I am forever grateful to each of them.

At SDSU, I grasped the golden ring of academia: I found an institutional home in the place I wanted to live. It is not hyperbole to say that I am blessed to work at SDSU and to be surrounded by colleagues like Phillip Serrato, Quentin Bailey, Bill Nericcio, Yetta Howard, Angel Matos, and Peter Herman, all of whom have read parts of this book and offered helpful suggestions on it. In particular, my colleague and dear friend Michael Borgstrom provided invaluable, incisive insights with grace and generosity, helping me see the big questions and also the reasons I should care about them.

My earliest readers of this project were colleagues at Yale: Caleb Smith, R. John Williams, Justin Neuman, and Jessica Brantley. Among those earliest trusted readers was Sam See. He left us far too early, and I miss him.

My most constant readers remain my graduate school buddies: Melissa Sodeman, Julia Lee, and Mark C. Marino. Mark has read every piece of this book, some parts many times. I thank him for his unique mixture of enthusiasm and endurance.

I have respected Rita Raley as a scholar since I was a graduate student and now count her as a friend. She provided astute critique of the book's arrangement at a vital time in its development, and the project is better for it.

Kiene Brillenburg Wurth has been on a partner in pursuing the ideas of this project and has become a great friend and travel companion along the way.

Other scholars I admire have given invaluable suggestions for research but also, and just as importantly, expressed confidence in my ability to pursue it at pivotal moments in the book's development. I thank Garrett Stewart, Matthew Kirschenbaum, Alan Liu, Leah Price, Lisa Gitelman, Paul St. Amour, and Daniel Tiffany for the bolster.

None of my scholarly work would be possible without the influence and guidance of my mentor, N. Katherine Hayles. I work to make her proud in every project and on every page.

I would never have finished this book if not for Rebecca Walkowitz. She expressed interest in the project far before it was a book, and her unwavering belief in it and in me—even when I thought I might leave the academy—kept me steadfast. Philip Leventhal stewarded this book to completion within incomparable patience and generous care as the best possible editor. Sarah Mesle entered in the final hours of this project, improving it with her brilliant pinch-editorial skills. I am grateful to them all.

Since this is a book about the networks of connection, attachment, and passion that enable and sustain literary culture, I want to acknowledge my dearest friends, Jennifer Guy and Pilar McLellan Dieter, for their constant support. I also want to acknowledge my teachers beyond the academy who have sustained me so that I could focus on books and bookishness: my ballet teachers Olga Tchekachova and Sayat Asatryan and my yoga teachers Kenna Crouch and Arielle Rabier Leon. The nonhuman actor that significantly influenced this project is Beacons Beach in Leucadia, where I would take my clipboard filled with printed-out chapters and edit by hand with my feet in the sand.

Finally, my greatest gratitude is to my family. My surname, Pressman, suggests a nearness to books. The "pressman" is the laborer in the print shop who maintains the printing press. As far as I know, the name "Pressman" was an Ellis Island concoction rather than a professional label. Regardless, my family has always loved books, revered learning, and respected the bookish. They have supported me in all of my academic endeavors, and I have no words to express my gratitude to them. My parents are models of how to live well; they love to learn and travel, love each other, and love life.

My husband, Brad, is my partner and best friend. I seek nearness to him over all books . . . and that is saying something.

Digital culture moves quickly, but scholarship does not. This book took me ten years to write. I was eight months pregnant with my daughter, Sydney, when I started this book; she is now ten years old and a reader in her own right. She and her older brother, Jonah (twelve), are the real objects of my affection. I dedicate this book to them with my deepest love.

BOOKISHNESS

INTRODUCTION

Bookishness is a twenty-first-century phenomenon, and it is omnipresent. Once you recognize it, you see it everywhere.

In the twenty-first century, we no longer *need* books, physical codices, as reading devices. We have other means of reading, writing, communicating, and archiving. But that doesn't mean some of us don't *want* books. And that want manifests everywhere. Indeed, at the moment of the book's foretold obsolescence because of digital technologies—around the turn of the millennium—we saw something surprising: the emergence of a creative movement invested in exploring and demonstrating love for the book as symbol, art form, and artifact.

This is what I describe as "bookishness": creative acts that engage the physicality of the book within a digital culture, in modes that may be sentimental, fetishistic, radical. Cell-phone covers crafted to look like old books; decorative pillows printed with beloved book covers; earrings, rings, and necklaces made of miniature codices; store windows that use books as props; altered book sculptures exhibited in prestigious collections; and bookbound novels that revolve around a book as a central character. Although the bookishness I will chart is primarily Anglophone, bookishness

FIGURE 0.1 Example of bookishness: Twelve South's BookBook for iPhone, a cell-phone cover crafted to look like an old book.

Source: Permission to use image granted by TwelveSouth.com.

happens across countries, languages, media, and genres. This obsession with the materiality of books spans the spectrum from high art to absolute kitsch, and it signifies a culture grappling with its own increasing digitization.

The book has historically symbolized privacy, leisure, individualism, knowledge, and power. This means that the book has been the emblem for the very experiences that must be renegotiated in a digital era: proximity, interiority, authenticity. So what happens when the books get digitized and bookish culture goes digital—when the word "book" may or may not refer to a material object? Bookishness signals a culture in transition but also provides a solution to a dilemma of the contemporary literary age: how to maintain a commitment to the nearness, attachment, and affiliation that the book traditionally represented now that the use value of the book has so

FIGURE 0.2 Example of bookishness: a headboard made from books.

Source: Permission to use image granted by Diycraftsy.com: https://www.diycraftsy.com/diy-headboard-ideas/.

radically altered. Books aren't going anywhere, but they are being repurposed and reimagined. Our relationships to books are changing, and often the results are surprisingly poetic and generative.

When I first started thinking about bookishness in 2008, I had to defend my claim of its existence. Ten years later, things have changed dramatically. Bookishness is now nearly inescapable. A few months ago, I encountered a wall of bookishness in a store at

FIGURE 0.3 Example of bookishness: necklace comprising
miniature books, by Peg and Awl.

Source: Accessed at Esty: https://www.etsy.com/listing/87301368/literary-book
-necklace-miniature-leather. Photo and necklace by Peg and Awl.
Permission to use image granted by Peg and Awl.

FIGURE 0.4 Example of bookishness: store window in New Orleans using books as decorations.

FIGURE 0.5 Example of bookishness: bookish cupcakes by Cakes and Cupcakes Mumbai.

Source: https://cakesandcupcakesmumbai.com/2013/01/13/book-lover-cakes -and-cupcakes/book-novels-lovers-cakes-cupcakes-mumbai-29/.

the Los Angeles International Airport: socks printed with the design of an old library card and titled "Out of Print / Books Worn well" hung above a box of "I Love Books" buttons sold with the tagline "Buttons for Book Lovers." This was all was displayed in a store that contained very few actual books and in a place where many people were reading but were doing so on their phones.

But the object that started it all for me was my Mac BookBook: a large brown leather computer case made to look like an old hardbound book. It is a beautiful and kitschy thing, and in 2010 it was a source of surprise to those who watched me unzip it and reveal a shiny silver laptop inside (see figure 0.6). There is also something sad about the Mac BookBook. Its presence signals an absence. Instead of pages and text, the hollowed-out codex is a storage device for a computer. It is the ultimate victory of simulacra over the original.[1] The Mac BookBook functions through indexical

FIGURE 0.6 Bookishness as laptop case: Twelve South's Mac BookBook.

Source: Permission to use image granted by TwelveSouth.com.

reference and a kind of spectral haunting. It makes books appear in places and scenes where they used to be physically present but are no longer. The cultural theorist Raymond Williams identified "the residual" as an important part of cultural formation. It is what "has been effectively formed in the past but is still active in the cultural process."[2] My Mac BookBook displays the book to be a powerful form of residual media actively shaping digital culture.[3]

Another point of origin for this book was the 2009 exhibit *Slash: Paper Under the Knife*, curated by Dave McFadden for the Museum of Art and Design in New York City. *Slash* featured fifty-two artists from sixteen countries, displaying "a virtual renaissance of interest in the use of paper as an independent medium beyond collage" and representing "an international phenomenon."[4] The exhibit captured well the cultural zeitgeist. Artists from around the world were shown to be exploring and exploiting the physical properties and aesthetic possibilities of paper and books. The book-based sculptures particularly riveted me. The medium of my profession (as an English professor) and personal passion (as a reader) was here treated as solid matter for making three-dimensional sculpture. *Slash* presented the book as a complex and compelling form of residual media, one that was being repurposed for new artistic shapes, sculptural forms, and aesthetic practices.

"Bookwork" is the term used to describe this genre of book-based sculpture. Artists such as Doug Beube, Brian Dettmer, Guy Laramée, Cara Barer, and Long Bin-Chen have made bookwork a signal genre of the digital age. It is a staple in contemporary exhibits and also proliferates on blogs and curated feeds across the internet. In bookwork, the book is presented as a physical thing of beauty, complexity, and fascination, not just as a storage container for text. We can't read the words contained in Pamela Paulsrud's *Touchstones* (books altered to look like small beach-tossed stones; see figure 0.7) or in Brian Dettmer's *New Funk Standards* because pieces of the pages have been cut away, shellacked, and otherwise altered (see figure 0.8).[5] Garrett Stewart identifies bookwork as a distinct genre of contemporary art in which the codex is "demediated," its medial function stripped away to become sculptural and aesthetic.[6] Stewart locates bookwork in a genealogy of conceptual and readymade art, thereby identifying bookwork as making us see books differently in order to reconsider what we expect from the concept, word, and image of "book."

It feels right to me that this exhibit of slashed and demediated books began the series of thoughts that would lead to this "book" I have written: a series of words that you, reader, may be finding on paper pages or may be encountering digitally in something called "page view." *Slash* lived up to its name. It slashed my way of seeing books and in doing so made me encounter books with a visceral,

FIGURE 0.7 Example of bookwork: Pamela Paulsrud's *Touchstones* (2013).

Source: https://pamelapaulsrud.com/artwork/197502_Touchstones.html.

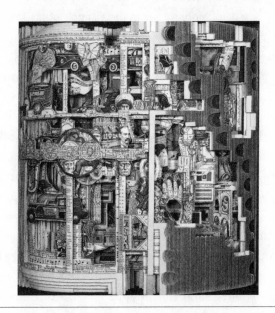

FIGURE 0.8 Example of bookwork: Brian Dettmer, *New Funk Standards* (2017), hardcover book, acrylic varnish, 12.75" × 12" × 5.75".

Source: Permission to use image granted by artist.

immediate force. It is that sense of immediacy, disrupted and enabled by the digital, that bookishness works to navigate.

Bookishness is about maintaining a nearness to books. "Bookishness" comes from "bookish," a word used to describe a person who reads a lot (perhaps too much). When coupled with "-ness," the term takes on a subtle new valence. The first listing of "-ishness" in the *Oxford English Dictionary* states that it derives from Old English, wherein "-ish" served chiefly to form adjectives from national names (British, English, Scottish); so "-ishness" is about identification, even nationalism. It is about subject formation through relationality, about locating and identifying a community of subjects in physical and spatial contexts. In this case, "bookishness" suggests an identity derived from a physical *nearness* to books, not just from the "reading" of them in the conventional sense. The "-ishness" also indicates that objects rub off on us. They affect us, opening interpretive modes. Moreover, as in the example of my Mac Book-Book, objects mark us—making us identifiable and even "readable" to others—as "bookish."

A few other objects from my personal collection of bookishness—objects I have used to mark myself, in my particular ways, as bookish—include a painting depicting a stack of closed books, a hanging mobile made from the *MLA Style Guide*, and a sculpture carved out of a hardbound *Moby-Dick* whose folded pages form the word "book." And there's a much wider swath of bookishness online: stop-motion book-based films, Pinterest sites dedicated to bookish fashion, Facebook communities that share photos of beautiful libraries around the world, and more . . . so much more. Collectively, these individual objects become representative of a larger movement and promote questions about what binds them. My survey of bookishness takes seriously the presence of these objects and the questions they promote about twenty-first-century digital life and meaning making.

Consider an example of bookishness kitsch that shows this meaning making in action: this *Pride and Prejudice* duvet cover (figure 0.9). How might we hold in view Jane Austen's classic novel *Pride and Prejudice* (1813) alongside a bedspread that references it? The duvet cover signifies one's knowledge of literary culture, and

FIGURE 0.9 Bookishness in the form of a duvet cover printed with bookshelves.

Source: https://www.cafepress.com/+bookshelf7100_queen_duvet,1103715894.

probably one's identification with this classic and much-commodified bildungsroman, but it does not guarantee that its owner has actually read the canonical novel.[7] Yet the duvet cover does serve to draw the novel (and literature more generally) through the commodity form and into the realm of the personal and affective, even the intimate space of the bedroom: to assert the attachment to books as a powerful form of self-making. And, when posted to social media, this bookish duvet cover also extends those private realms into cyberspace. Much like the Great Books of the Western World series or the hardbound encyclopedia sets that filled the bookshelves of mid-twentieth-century bourgeois American living rooms, bookishness is about class and consumerism. It is about constructing and projecting identity through the possession and presentation of books. The difference here is that unlike the shelf of leather-bound but never-opened canonical texts, books no longer need to be owned or physically displayed in order to do the work of self-construction. Digital images posted to social media now serve that purpose. They help to maintain a "nearness" to books in a digital realm that is becoming ever more an extension of our intimate living and personal spaces, a process that makes evaluating what counts as "near" ever more complex.

Another way to consider the stakes of bookishness might be to reverse the seeming "literariness" of my example. If we might ask about the relation of the words that make up the story *Pride and Prejudice* to the representation of *Pride and Prejudice* on a bedspread, we might equally ask what it means when we find a character in a novel reading *Pride and Prejudice* or discover diverse adaptations of the classic story updated for contemporary times (a Muslim version, a gay version, etc.).[8] Neither the duvet cover nor the words "Pride and Prejudice" are the book *Pride and Prejudice*; instead, the bedspread and the beloved novel, I would say, combine to serve as examples of bookishness. Put differently, we see bookishness *in* the books we read; it is a literary mode even as it is also a way to com-modify (as in the duvet cover) literariness. From avant-garde experimental literature to best-selling middlebrow fiction, "chick lit" to children's storybooks, contemporary literature depicts the book as a central character in narrative plots and also plays with the aesthetic possibilities of the codexical format. Even born-digital literature, a genre with no physical allegiance to the codex, gets in on the bookishness game. Electronic literature adapts the appear-ance of books into screen-based poetics and incorporates actual books into augmented-reality, transmedial storytelling.

Bookishness pervades nonliterary books too. Consider *The Repurposed Library: 33 Craft Projects That Give Old Books New Life* by Lisa Occhipinti, with photography by Thayer Allyson Gowdy. A "how-to" book for wannabe bookwork artists, *The Repurposed Library* presents the book as physical material for making things: shelves, hanging mobiles, bracelets, birdhouses, wreathes for the front door, chande-liers, vases, sculpture, and more. Occhipinti's introduction begins with an act of not-reading: "As a child I adored books, despite the fact that I hated to read." She describes seeking out her mother's family Bible: "I wouldn't read a word, but I would marvel at the translucent, onionskin pages and the faux shagreen cover embossed with gilt letters." A self-proclaimed book lover but not book reader, Occhipinti writes, "Repurposing a book is simply a different way of experiencing it and embracing its beauty." Her introduction to *The Repurposed Library* concludes with the promise that her book will alter your view of books in general, in effect holding on to interpre-tation and evaluation as bookish processes that are quite separate from "reading": "You won't look at them the same way again."[9] Bookishness, in general, performs this same trick—although not always to the same nonreading ends—promoting an appreciation of the physical book in, through, and against an orientation toward the digital.

Such lessons are not just for adults. Children's literature also uses bookishness to share and teach a love of books' materiality, even for those who might appreciate other forms of reading and writing. Lane Smith's *It's a Book* is a short picture book for young readers. It depicts a monkey reading a book while an annoying donkey asks him questions about it. The donkey represents the digital native, and for him the book is a strange device. "Do you blog with it?" the donkey asks; "No, it's a book," says the monkey. More questions ensue: "Does it need a password?" The monkey repeats the refrain: "No, it's a book."[10] The question-and-answer session continues until the donkey finally takes a turn with the book. He holds it in his hands and gets hooked. The book's final page depicts the donkey immersed in a book while a little mouse (a character, not an interactive device) delivers the pedagogical punch line. The donkey, still not fully understanding how a book works but evidently smitten with it nonetheless, promises to charge it when he's finished reading. The mouse responds: "You don't have to . . . it's a book, Jackass." The joke inculcates young readers into a bookish set, elevating those who get the joke and who love books apart from those jackasses who prefer digital devices.

Hervé Tullet's *Press Here* is another example of a popular children's book that teaches young readers to see the book as a powerful and compelling medium, particularly in relation to interactive screens.[11] *Press Here* begins with a yellow dot and the words "press here and turn the page" in a font that resembles handwriting. The next page displays two yellow dots, sitting side by side. The words "Great! Now press the yellow dot again" appear underneath. The text infers an interactive reading experience (à la a touchscreen device), rewarding the reader for her action of presumably pressing the dot and turning the page afterward. Of course, there is no actual change in content on the book's pages, regardless of readerly action. The reader knows this and plays along, and the play is part of the fun. *Press Here* references the digital in an act of parody with a pedagogical purpose: it teaches the young reader to play with the book and to appreciate it, endearing the reader to the codexical medium. This lesson is an introduction in being bookish, but it depends upon familiarity with interactive screens. *Press Here*, like *It's a Book*, reorients young readers toward the book medium through a relationship with the digital. Such literature reinforces a sense of being bookish in a digital age and for digital natives.

WHY NOW?

Bookishness speaks to and from a particular historical moment. From 2000 to 2015, the period of my investigation, a lot happened to our relationship to the book and, more generally, to how we get information and entertainment and establish bookish communities. During this time, we saw the emergence of Google (taking off in 2000), Wikipedia (2001), Web 2.0 (2004), social media platforms (Facebook in 2004, Twitter in 2006, Instagram in 2010), Google Books (2005), and the general acceptance of constantly connected mobile devices that dramatically transform our everyday lived experience into a culture of "always on."[12] The Kindle arrived in 2007, the most successful in a longer genealogy of e-readers that preceded it, and reading on a digital device became popular and pervasive.[13]

A 2008 *New York Times* article works as a useful benchmark for my study; its title alone speaks volumes about the impact of these rapid technological changes on what it means to be bookish: "Literacy Debate: Online, R U Really Reading?" The article begins with a large color photograph of an upper-middle-class family sitting in their stately living room in Old Greenwich, Connecticut—a vision of bourgeois bliss and simultaneous domestic conflict wrought by the digital. Father reads the newspaper and mother a book while each kid has a MacBook on his and her lap. The photo caption reads, "The Simses of Old Greenwich, Conn., gather to read after dinner. Their means of text delivery is divided by generation."[14] The image replicates older gendered norms associated with reading: the man/ father reads the newspaper while the woman/mother curls up with a book. Her physical position implies that, unlike her husband, who studies the objective news, she is engrossed in a novel. The gender norms at work in this scene of reading suggest a history of normative values associated with literary media that are being transferred to a new site of conflict: print versus digital.

The pairing of the photo with the article's title expresses anxiety about reading in an increasingly digital age. The first two lines focus this concern on the children: "Books are not Nadia Konyk's thing. Her mother, hoping to entice her, brings them home from the library, but Nadia rarely shows an interest." The article establishes a generational divide based on reading devices, a conflict that's carried out via a synecdoche that depends on bookishness: while the title asks a question about reading, the first lines synecdochally transfer the activity (reading) to the object (the physical book). In 2008, a year after the advent of the Kindle, the idea of reading a book digitally was still surprising. The article expresses a commonly felt apprehension that family members might be unable to share knowledge and a sense of cultural history because, according to the logic of the article's title, reading on a screen just might not count as reading at all.

Yet only two years later—in 2010—the *New York Times* announced that the paper would include an e-book bestseller list in fiction and nonfiction.[15] In other words, only two years after publishing the article about the Simses, the *New York Times* changed course. Today, the image of the Simses sitting together with different reading devices probably no longer strikes fear in the hearts of those concerned about the future of books, reading, and a common core of knowledge. It is now possible to imagine the young Simses, on their digital devices, reading titles suggested by the reputable *New York Times Book Review*.

Fears about the death of the book, which pervaded and book-ended (as it were) the turn of the century, have subsided a bit. If we think back to the year 1999, specifically to the hysteria surrounding the approach of January 1, 2000, we can see how much has changed in cultural attitudes toward digital technologies. Y2K, as the year 2000 was called, laid bare primal fears about the transition to a digital culture. There was the Y2K bug, a computer error projected to create havoc in computer systems globally because of a flaw in representing dates beyond December 31, 1999. It ended up doing little actual technological damage but did expose how a seemingly small technical concern could potentially affect global markets, transportation systems, and the cultural imagination.

Such fears may seem wild and far off now; two decades into the twenty-first century, people seem all too willing to trust their personal data to the unseen but significantly named "cloud" and to submit regularly to corporate privacy-setting policies in exchange for faster online service and sleeker apps.[16] We have accepted omnipresent computing and corporate surveillance into our homes and most intimate contexts—our mobile phones, cars, refrigerators, watches, and, yes, even our reading devices. Computers are now a central and culturally accepted reading platform. And not only are e-readers such as Kindles and Nooks (introduced in 2007 by Amazon and in 2009 by Barnes & Noble, respectively) sold alongside books at bookstores, but data also shows that the sales of digital releases can increase, not diminish, the sale of printed books.[17] The contemporary situation is not a binary of print versus digital or books versus screens. We face something far more complex and interesting.

The period of this book's study also encompasses dramatic shifts in book publishing. Innovations in digital techniques for book design, color and typographic printing, die-cuts, and other page elements go hand in hand with new capacities for augmented-reality elements and transmedial storytelling as well as digitally enhanced advertising and distribution modes. The digital is now a staple of book publishing, from the creation of content on word-processing software to the point-of-sale scanning of ISBNs as digital barcodes. N. Katherine Hayles rightly claims that "digitality has become the textual condition of twenty-first century literature."[18] Printed bookbound novels and the readers who buy them are, whether they realize it, affected by major shifts in digital production and corporate "convergence culture" that have revolutionized the film, television, and, of course, book-publishing industries.[19] Just think of how Amazon.com (originally marketed as a bookseller) is now a producer of television and film. The effects of these changes are seen and felt in the books we read and also in how they arrive at our front door: in a brown box with a big, black, arrow-pointed smile from Amazon.com.

Amazon.com went online in 1995; its effects on bookselling might be compared—in the scale of influence and the complexity of interaction—to the rise of the digital on books. The changes represented by this one company (even this one word, "Amazon") are well known both in lived experience and in cultural history. During the fifteen years of my study, Amazon.com became a giant. In 2019, it is ranked as the third-largest company in the world by market value.[20] Amazon.com was blamed for the death of the brick-and-mortar bookstore and then started opening its own storefronts (in 2015). Indeed, I would argue that the recent resurgence of bookstores is evidence of bookishness at work.

The literary scholar Mark McGurl queries, "Should Amazon.com now be considered the driving force of American literary history?"[21]

Even if the answer is not a certain "yes," then at least we must acknowledge that Amazon.com is one of the main driving forces of contemporary literary culture. Not only do many people find, buy, read, and recommend books via the online "everything store," but Amazon.com is more and more becoming the mediatized environment through which we encounter and experience the literary more broadly. The example of Amazon.com shows how and why we must read across and between that kitschy Jane Austen duvet cover and her canonical bookbound novel. Both are found and purchased on the same website, where they are programmatically connected by metatags, hyperlinks, and more. This technical situation invites us to pay attention to the attachments between these literary objects and, beyond them, the relationships that constitute the literary in this new media world.

MY METHOD

In the chapters that follow, I pursue bookishness across diverse texts, objects, and aesthetics. I suture methods from literary studies, book history, and media studies. I take inspiration from Marshall McLuhan and Quentin Fiore's very bookish book from 1967, *The Medium Is the Massage*, which proclaims to be "a look-around to see what's happening. It is a collide-oscope of interfaced situations."[22] I adopt a kaleidoscopic perspective, collecting and curating an array of texts and genres into constellations that, through their arrangement, show us something new about how and why we continue to love books in a digital age.

Media studies, particularly media-specific analysis and media archaeology, support my efforts.[23] Indeed, my goal is to show how the literary and literariness are reliant on our digital network, our technologies, and also habits of use. I heed Craig Dworkin's warning: "We are misled when we think of media as objects."[24] Approaching literary culture through a media perspective means thinking not just about objects or subjects—texts, books, readers, authors, genres—but also about the relationships, networks, and infrastructures that constitute and connect them. Similarly, as David Thorburn and Henry Jenkins suggest: "To comprehend the aesthetics of transition, we must resist notions of media purity, recognizing that each medium is touched by and in turn touches its neighbors and rivals."[25] Applied to literary studies, we must approach texts as media operating within specific networks of connection and "touch." I am moved by Rita Felski's call to reorganize literary critical practice around attachment rather than detachment—to think seriously about how literary objects are actors (to "acknowledge poems and paintings, fictional characters and narrative devices, as actors").[26] "If literary studies is to survive the twenty-first century," Felski writes, "it will need to reinvigorate its ambitions and its methods by forging closer links to the study of other media rather than clinging to ever more tenuous claims to exceptional status."[27] Bookishness generates such links, for example, those between Melville's *Moby-Dick* and my Isaac Salazar-folded bookwork made from it. In the digital network, such attachment is not just affective and aesthetic but also programmatic and enacted. Hyperlinks connect webpages, and metadata tags and search-engine cookies foster connections between bits of bookish data. Invisible algorithms enable a user's search-engine history to generate new, perhaps adjacently related bookish content and—of course—potential purchases. A focus on bookishness illuminates where and how the literary works now.

Attachment, pleasure, disgust, intrigue, and play are all important parts of the literary and deserve to be understood as such. These are reasons why we read, study, teach, share, and own books. I am indebted (and attached) to work by literary critics like Leah

Price and Andrew Piper, who think about the role of the book, past and present, as well as Deidre Shauna Lynch, whose *Loving Literature: A Cultural History*, shows how Literature (with a capital L) developed into a serious discipline and object of study during the eighteenth century due to a nexus of cultural efforts that collectively turned bookbound literature into something to love. Lynch writes: "Recovering the historicity of the love of literature" means "tracing a counterplot to those orthodox accounts of the development of aesthetics, since these tend to make, not attachment but detachment their end point."[28] A focus on bookishness shows how the digital inspires literary innovation around an emergent bookish sensibility. My hope is that this book shows the literary—and literary criticism, too—to be flourishing, perhaps even having a kind of renaissance in and, indeed, because of our digital age.

THE CHAPTERS

The chapters that follow examine bookishness as a complex constellation of technological, social, aesthetic, and affective forces that converge to present the book as aesthetic artifact par excellence for our digital culture. Chapter 1, "How and Now Bookishness," situates bookishness historically, explaining how bookishness emerged as a response to anxieties and rhetoric about the death of the book in the 1990s. Chapter 2, "Shelter," explores how these fears get enacted in narratives that share a central trope: the presentation of the book as an allegorical outpost, a safe space and shelter. Across a wide variety of narratives—Jennifer Egan's mystery novel *The Keep* (2006); the 9/11 novels *The Zero* (2006), by Jess Walter, and *Extremely Loud & Incredibly Close* (2005), by Jonathan Safran Foer; William Joyce's children's book *The Fantastic Flying Books of Mr. Morris Lessmore* (2012); and Robin Sloane's page-turner

Mr. Penumbra's 24-Hour Bookstore (2012)—we see a central goal of bookishness emerge as an effort to depict the book allegorically as a space of refuge from an encroaching digital world.

Bookishness affects literature not only at the level of content and story but also in form and format. Chapter 3, "Thing," examines bookishness literature that depicts the book as a thing, a poignant artifact and fetish object for the digital age. In diegetic narrative and in formal presentation, these works take advantage of digital publishing and production capacities to focus readerly attention on the beauty and power of the book object. Leanne Shapton's *Important Artifacts and Personal Property from the Collection of Lenore Doolan and Harold Morris, Including Books, Street Fashion, and Jewelry* (2009) is a unique little book that presents a narrative in the form of an auction catalogue. Objects left over from a romantic relationship are used to tell the story of a human relationship and reflexively comment on the power of the book as artifact and archive. Carlos María Domínguez's *The House of Paper* (2005) and Amaranth Borsuk and Brad Bouse's augmented-reality work *Between Page and Screen* (2012) are very different texts, one print and one digital, but both adapt an older literary genre that fetishizes and anthropomorphizes the book object into a narrative actor. Sean and Lisa Ohlenkamp's short stop-motion film *The Joy of Books* (2012) exemplifies a genre of bookishness that proliferates online and depicts the book as thing coming to life, thereby animating the very definition of fetish object by depicting the book as an important fetish object for a literary culture dependent upon digital infrastructures.

Digital technologies enable intricate book design and cheap, mass-produced quantities of bookish beauty but also piracy, fakery, and knockoffs. Chapter 4, "Fake," shows how digital culture operates through fakery—an essential cultural value that, like nearness, is interrupted by the digital—and, specifically, how the contemporary literary condition is indebted to bookish remediations and kitsch. From digital files presented as books to "blooks" (objects made to look like books), dummy spines to bookish kitsch, I consider bookish fakes as an important aspect of literary culture. I read examples of bookishness kitsch in relation to two novels that operate through the conceit of bookish fakery: J. J. Abrams and Doug Dorst's *S.* (2013) and *The Ice-Bound Concordance* (2016), by Aaron A. Reed and Jacob Garbe, an augmented-reality narrative game. Fakery is part of the literary, both literature's past and its present, and bookishness provides an opportunity to consider the importance of fake books to our bookish future.

My final two chapters adopt a different method, shifting from demonstrating through curation to close reading one or two literary examples. Chapter 5, "Weapon," considers the role of experimental literature and book design within bookishness by diving into two exemplary novels, Mark Z. Danielewski's *House of Leaves* (2000) and Steven Hall's *The Raw Shark Texts* (2007). These highly experimental novels play with the materiality of the book to present narrative allegories that figure the digital as monstrous and the book as a powerful weapon against it. *House of Leaves* exploits the possibilities of the codex in ways that demonstrate its durability and phoenix-like ability to regenerate. *The Raw Shark Texts* uses typographical play and a mind-bending plot to critique posthuman theories that disentangle information from materiality, self from body. Both of these texts were origin points of sorts for the book you're now reading. Returning to them, we can see how they registered aspects of early fears about the digital and established an aesthetic of bookishness as a response.

Bookishness registers a sense of loss and promotes remembrance. Chapter 6, "Memorial," addresses the memorializing function of bookishness by examining a single, exemplary work: Jonathan Safran Foer's *Tree of Codes* (2010). A memorial and fetish object for bookish culture, *Tree of Codes* is full of holes—gaps in the page that are aesthetic and deeply meaningful. Foer employed a digitally enhanced process of die-cutting to carve into an English-language edition of the Polish author Bruno Schulz's *The Street of Crocodiles* (1934), creating a beautiful, hole-y, and very bookish thing from it. Schulz died during the Holocaust, and his writing was largely lost to history. The sense of loss—the loss of people, books, and cultural memory—permeates *Tree of Codes*, figuratively and formally. I read *Tree of Codes* as a memorial not only to Schulz and the Holocaust but also to bookish culture in the twenty-first century. Reading attentively the experimental pages of Foer's *Tree of Codes*, we see bookishness registering and memorializing a time of signal change in literary culture—our own.

This book ends with a short and rather personal "Coda" that attends to the feelings motivating my thoughts (and years of research) on bookishness. Loving books in a digital age is personal and communal, especially since those distinctions are being blurred by digital infrastructures and cultural practices. As our lives and loves depend increasingly upon the digital, we literary critics need to be attuned to how feelings matter to the literary and also to literary criticism.

In the end, loving books is about attachment. This is especially true in a digital age because digital culture operates through attachment, through networks of hyperlinks and programmatic connections. But it's more than that. In our neoliberal times, in which digital corporations invade our private space and reading time, claiming a bookish identity can constitute an act of rebellion, self-construction, and hope *within* this sphere.

May the book that you hold in your hands strengthen your own attachments to the literary and support reflection on why loving books matters so much now.

1

HOW AND NOW BOOKISHNESS

In the years leading up to the new millennium, fears of the digital were articulated as threats to the book. Rhetoric about the death of book proliferated and spurred a response in the form of bookishness.

THE DEATH OF THE BOOK

The book was not always under threat—often the book itself *was* the threat. In a pivotal scene in *The Hunchback of Notre Dame* (1831), set in fifteenth-century Paris during the emergence of the printing press, Victor Hugo poses the archdeacon Claude Frollo, the narrative embodiment of the Catholic Church, alongside a book and a view of Notre Dame: "The archdeacon gazed at the gigantic edifice for some time in silence, then extending his right hand, with a sigh, towards the printed book which lay open on the table, and his left towards Notre-Dame, and turning a sad glance from the book to the church,—'Alas,' he said, 'this will kill that.' "[1] The statement "this will kill that" expresses a belief that new media (here, the book) will destroy older, established forms of knowledge production and distribution (here, the church).

History shows that fears about new media "killing" older ones say more about the changing social contexts and power structures of the time than about actual readers, books, or literary practices. Five hundred years after Gutenberg's invention, we have become used to books as accessible, ever-present commodities and personal comforts. We forget that the book was once the new media raising concern about its potential power. Indeed, even before the printing press revolutionized the manufacture of books, cultural critics feared the impact of the codex. In 1525, Erasmus wrote, "Is there anywhere on earth exempt from these swarms of new books?"[2] He continues, expressing anxieties about how emergent literacy and the presence of books will "fill the world with pamphlets and books [that are] . . . foolish, ignorant, malignant, libelous, mad, impious and subversive; and such is the flood that even things that might have done some good lose all their goodness."

I begin with these examples because they anticipate so clearly—in their tone, their concerns, and their intelligent misapprehension—familiar accounts about the media shift of our own era. Hugo's archbishop was clearly wrong that the printed book would kill the church (though it did significantly affect its power and how it exercised it), but he was not wrong that the book would be what Elizabeth Eisenstein, in her history of the printing press, famously calls "an agent of change."[3] Early responses to the rise of digitization share with these earlier writers a tone of lament that is incorrect in its hyperbole—the book has not died any more than the church did—but also correct in its expressive estimation of digitization's impact. Bookishness literature learns from this history, updating the idea that the book can serve as a weapon and reminding us of its power.

Leah Price rightly states, "Every generation rewrites the book's epitaph; all that changes is the whodunit."[4] In the early stages of thinking about bookishness, I considered writing a history of "the death of the book" genre, focusing on its rhetorical practices and assumptions.[5] Approaching the death of the book as a distinct (and reoccurring) discursive genre invites consideration of how and why that genre operates, not just whether it is right or wrong. Bookishness is a response to the most recent bout of claims about the death of the book at the hands (or digits) of the digital, and as such it invites us to return to the particular cultural conversation about the death of the book that flourished at the turn of the last century. The melancholy expressed in this conversation is not "right," in that it does not reflect an accurate historical awareness of the media (which to say, the book) it longs for, nor does it register any perspicacity in predicting the media future. Yet the tenor and content of this discourse express a powerful set of values that's worthwhile for us to understand.

Two of the period's most famous laments about books in the digital age are Sven Birkets's *The Gutenberg Elegies* (1994) and Nicolas Carr's "Is Google Making Us Stupid?" (2008), a pairing that bookends the year 2000. These two highly influential and often-cited texts share certain operating assumptions.[6] "My core fear is that we, as a culture, are becoming shallower," Birkets writes.[7] Fifteen years later, after the emergence of Web 2.0, Carr concurs: "Once I was a scuba diver in the sea of words. Now I zip along the surface like a guy on a jet ski."[8] In both accounts, digital media promote the wrong kind of reading: not deep, linear, and immersive but instead shallow, hyperlinked skimming. Hear the depth metaphors at work. Associated with literary criticism since at least (and informed by) Freud, the depth model of reading understands good, serious reading to be an act of excavating subtexts and hidden meaning.[9] For both Birkets and Carr, computational culture produces a shift from reading as deep diving to superficial skimming of the surface. The results, our representative hand-wringers note, are not for the better. These familiar rationales yoke the book medium to a particular method of use (linear reading) and to a particular value (good). They see the internet as the opposite. Birkets and Carr build their claims about the death of books and bookish values upon the following assumptions: books are for reading; reading is beneficial, especially when it is done in a linear, immersive fashion; and books and literature are one and the same.

Yet even as they praise slow, careful thinking, the rationale posited by Birkets, Carr, and others lacks, perhaps predictably, any deep understanding of media or book history.[10] While it is not my aim to seek to disprove a set of writers whose ideas are already outdated, it's useful to compare the ahistorical and ideological *idea* of the book they present to the reality of the book we can find in media histories. The first assumption—that books are for reading—is dispelled in Leah Price's *How to Do Things with Books in Victorian England*, which charts the many ways a person in nineteenth-century Britain might use a book: the book as an object to share and shape relationships between people, the book as an obstacle to shield oneself from others in the pursuit of private space, and the book as raw material to take to the privy.[11] In Price's history, reading becomes one among many embodied encounters with books, and certainly not the most intimate. The second foundational assumption undergirding Birkets's and Carr's death-of-the-book claims—that reading is beneficial—crumbles under the analysis of Deidre Shauna Lynch, among others, who describes that assumption as "neither inevitable nor historically constant."[12] Victorian fears about the dangerous physical and mental effects young women faced because of their novel reading—the very kind of immersive reading Birkets and Carr praise—are just one familiar point of evidence that reading has never been understood as good for all people.

Assuming that reading is good when it is done in a linear, immersive fashion rather than, say, in a jet-ski-like skimming is also ahistorical. Peter Stallybrass argues that the major innovation of the book over the scroll was the ability to skip around in it.[13] The book, in other words, was the first random-access reading machine. The third assumption—that books and literature are one and the same—is just historically inaccurate. Reading from cover to cover in a linear fashion, generating a form of literary escapism, is actually a relatively new and still comparatively small part of reading practice.[14] The media scholar Lisa Gitelman has shown that literature, especially the novel, is only a minuscule part of printed materials, even printed reading materials.[15] In other words, it is *not* that reading is at risk or that books are in threat of demise but rather that certain cherished associations about books are being challenged in our new media age.

My second example of rhetoric about the death of the book in this turn-of-the-millennium period comes not from individual pundits but from a national institution. In 2004, the National Endowment for the Arts released the report "Reading at Risk," a document that has since become a cultural touchstone.[16] The report drew from large-scale surveys conducted by the Census Bureau in 2002, and it concluded that people were reading less literature and also that the United States will suffer because of this. "For the first time in modern history, less than half of the adult population now reads literature, and these trends reflect a larger decline in other sorts of reading," the NEA's chairman, Dana Gioia, writes in his preface to the report. "Anyone who loves literature or values the cultural, intellectual, and political importance of active and engaged literacy in American society will respond to this report with grave concern."[17] Responses to the report were swift and cutting. Some critics pointed out the flaws in the report's analysis and interpretation—and many even at the time saw the cultural and ideological underpinnings at play in the NEA's ahistorical and universalizing document. The linguist Geoffrey Nunberg, for example, retorts, "But let's get real. The people who have been lost to novel reading aren't the dévo-tés of great literature"; what is at risk "isn't the monuments of West-ern literature, but only the leisure activity that we describe as 'curl-ing up with a good book.' "[18] Nunberg points out that leisure time, and the sensibility that one should use such time to read a novel, is a class privilege and predilection. What is at stake in calling such changes "risks" has less to do with reading per se than with changes to who gets to read (that is, who has leisure time and class privilege).

Other responses to the NEA report took issue with its underlying assumption that a decrease in reading *print* literature means a decrease in reading literature more generally. Matthew Kirschen-baum, writing on behalf of the Electronic Literature Organization, explains, "Electronic media need not put literary reading at risk; in fact once we begin taking screens as well as pages seriously as venues for literature and written expression, organizations such as the NEA may well find that rates of literacy are again on the rise."[19] What is at risk, in Kirschenbaum's account, is not the end of read-ing or the death of books but changes in reading practices, readerly publics, and the material constitution of literature. New types of literature (including electronic literature, video games, and fan fic-tion) and new ways of reading (including reading across hyper-linked, networked sites) may threaten older presumptions of what "literature" and "reading" mean but do not mean the end a literary (or literate) republic.

Whether or not one concludes from the NEA report that read-ing is actually at risk in the digital age, the report represented a signal moment in literary and bookish culture: it articulated a sense of cultural concern for the sea change underway caused by digital media. It was part of the cultural landscape that stimulated bookishness.

Twenty years into the new millennium, some effects of that sea change are becoming apparent. We have new authorial voices accessed through new modalities of content production and distribution. We have new markets and business models for the literary, new modes of review culture, and new platforms to support them. We even have new college courses to address these new forms. Simone Murray writes, "Literary culture has become a complex hybrid of print and digital outlets that exist in a state of mutual dependence."[20] This mutuality upsets the conceptual binary of print versus digital, which provided the foundation for fears about the death of the book around the year 2000. The situation is more complex than "this will kill that," and the concerns it signals are more far-reaching.

Changes in readership (who gets to read and who reads what), changes in literacy (both literacy rates and also qualifications about what counts as "literate"), changes in authority and authorial copyright, and of course changes in class boundaries and relationships entwined with these issues all propel contemporary rhetoric about the death of the book. Whose power might be threatened with changes to the established, print-based infrastructures that support literary values, publishing practices, academic institutions, and more? Who gets to be bookish and concerned about the death of the book in our digital age? Is it the white middle-class elite? Those with capitalized letters after their names, NPR listeners, devotees of independent bookstores, or some other group? A central argument of this book is that bookishness promotes such reflection because it directs our attention beyond hand-wringing over media obsolescence to questions of why we care. The changes the digital era has wrought in our lived experience—our habits, our schedules, our temporalities—shape how we feel about books, so looking at those feelings and their bookish emblems and practices shows us the contours of life in the digital age.[21]

THE BOOK

Thinking about *how* and *why* we care about books in a digital age requires us to think critically and historically about the object, symbol, and signifier at the heart of this issue. Even before Erasmus wrote anxiously about the book's ability to mislead and distract, the book had evolved into *the* symbol in Western culture of knowledge, selfhood, and the sacred. We learn to see ourselves in books and to understand ourselves through interactions with them. We are interpellated into becoming selves and subjects through books.[22] It is thus understandable that, in a digital moment, "As our shelves emptied out, we feared losing our selves."[23] The book is also a symbol of and a tool for producing a particular type of learned subject. "Certainly the object that most pervasively does culture to us, imposes or instills it, or at least did for most of modernity, is the bound print book."[24] The "us" here is important: Western, Judeo-Christian, middle class or at least instilled with ideals of bourgeois mobility. "Books are more than repositories of text; they are icons of knowledge."[25] The book has been used as a tool for learning and also for training the liberal human subject to know herself and know who she wants to become.[26]

For all these reasons, the book has been a powerful tool of Western power and colonization.[27] "The printed book was one of the most effective means of mastery over the whole world."[28] The successful spread of Christianity depended in part upon the book's format and the emergence of an iconography of the book as the word of God.[29] So too did Manifest Destiny and white, Christian power in the United States depend upon practices of alternately denying access to books (especially to people of color) and using them as a rationale or means for conquest. The promise and threat that the book medium can upend the status quo and threaten established power is part of its history. That is why nostalgia for the book in the age of its supposed obsolescence is distinct from nostalgia for other kinds of older media like vinyl records, typewriters, fountain pens, or nearly anything else.[30] The history of the book is about power and politics, so its contemporary fetishization through bookishness demands analysis in that register.

The book has been used to control other people and also to control one's own sense of self. For centuries, "bookish" has registered Enlightenment ideals about the liberal human subject—an individual in possession of himself, a tabula rasa or white page open to education and social uplift via books.[31] This nearness to books is not always positive. Just recall Emerson's warning in "The American Scholar" (1837) about becoming too bookish: "instead of Man Thinking, we have the bookworm"; and, of course, his beautiful adage, "Books are the best of things, well used; abused, among the worst."[32] Or, consider how "bookish," when associated with young female readers in Victorian England, presumed pernicious improprieties: curling up with a book suggested a form of intellectual and physical masturbation.[33] Or, of course, we can return to arguably the first modern novel and see it as warning about reading too much and being too bookish: Miguel de Cervantes's *Don Quixote* (1605 and 1615) follows a reader of romances who gets so carried away by the fiction he reads that he can no longer recognize reality. We use books to develop and project identities. In fact, we learn to do so from books themselves. Think of the moment in F. Scott Fitzgerald's *The Great Gatsby* (1925) when we see Gatsby's library of uncut, and therefore unread, books. Gatsby hopes the books will demonstrate his wealth and attest to the success of this upwardly mobile, self-made man, but the narrator suggests to the reader that this idea of bookish power is flawed.

Proclaiming the self through the shelf goes back at least to Buonaccorso da Montemagno's fourteenth-century treatise *Controversia de nobilitate*. As Bonnie Mak shows, this story of a suitor vying for the hand of his beloved, even though he does not possess the class or capital to compete for her hand, demonstrates how "books can attest to the character of their owner."[34] The suitor owns an impressive personal library, and the collection stands in to function as "a theatrical space of self-exhibition, a monument and a memorial to study."[35] The bookshelves serve as evidence that the noble pursuit of knowledge can offer an alternative to a noble birth. *Controversia de nobilitate* depicts bookshelves as a means of self-fashioning and self-representation, and books become equated with social mobility (as in Gatsby). So, what happens when we own Kindles or Nooks and rent, borrow, or store books in the cloud, rather than own their physical forms? How do we then project our constructed bookish selves out into the world?

A *New York Times* article from 2009 (in the wake of the introduction of the Kindle in 2007) addresses this question. Its provocative and telling title says it all: "With Kindle, Can You Tell It's Proust?" The article builds upon an understanding that books are barometers for self-fashioning and community construction as it blithely suggests the potential fallouts of e-readers:

> The practice of judging people by the covers of their books is old and time-honored. And the Kindle, which looks kind of like a giant white calculator, is the technology equivalent of a plain brown wrapper. If people jettison their book collections or stop buying new volumes, it will grow increasingly hard to form snap opinions about them by wandering casually into their living rooms.[36]

When we can longer judge others by the books they carry, how do we find (and avoid) one another? Like other aspects of contemporary literary culture, this too moves online.

"Shelfies"—the bookish version of the selfie—is a self-portrait in front of one's bookshelves or a photograph of the books on one's shelves. Thousands of shelfies can be found on social media. Just "type in 'shelfie' on Instagram and 582K posts appear," a fact that leads a *Telegraph* journalist to conclude, "The self-obsessed are also shelf-obsessed."[37] Whether bibliographies or aspirational reading lists, shelfies serve to project a bookish self-image out into the digital sphere. Digital self-making has become as versatile a practice as digital reading, and shelfies have emerged as important citation devices for producing bookish identities and communities.[38] The shelfie is just the latest configuration of equating books and selves and of judging others by their (virtual) bookshelves. Its presence registers the importance of the book as a particular type of object: a metonym for the self. The point is that bookish practices of self-construction persist. We need to look to the digital to understand the bookish.

As the example of the shelfie shows, our contemporary relationships to books happen as much through virtual bookshelves as through physical ones. One way of understanding how and why bookishness happens now is to look at the most famous example of a digital bookshelf. In 2010, Apple launched iBooks, and the interface design for this tablet-based program is a now-iconic bookshelf (see figure 1.1). This bookish design exemplifies bookishness because it enables a feeling of nearness to books where physical books and bookshelves do not exist. Let us take a quick look at the iBook interface to see what it can tell us about why bookishness is a distinctly twenty-first-century phenomenon.

The virtual bookshelf displays books with their covers, rather than spines, facing outward. This is a move that brick-and-mortar bookstores are now mimicking, a fact that reminds us that old and new media operate in complex loops of recursive influence rather

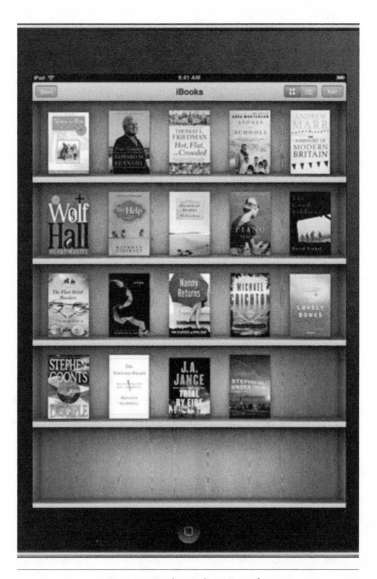

FIGURE 1.1 Apple iBook app interface.

Source: https://www.the-ebook-reader.com/ibooks.html.

than in a linear "this will kill that" model.[39] Henry Petroski has shown how changes in bookshelf design expose more than just the evolution of a particular storage technology: they signal changes in cultural values about knowledge and power. When books were first arranged in rows on shelves, in the Middle Ages, they were placed with the spines turned inward. Books were then handmade and extremely precious; they had clasps to keep the parchment pages from wrinkling and were chained to shelves to keep the books from disappearing.[40] This was also far before public libraries, so each library had its own locating system, and the select patrons of these libraries knew the content and the locating system. When innovations in printing technologies expanded book production, libraries became public, and literacy rates swelled; bookshelves registered the changes. For example, the Dewey Decimal System (c. 1876 in the United States) imprinted bibliographic data on the book's spine, so that part of the book was most useful to face the reader/user. The iBook interface presents and organizes books not through the traditions of card catalogues and standard bibliographies (with the text-based content of title, author, publisher, date, etc.) but instead around book cover art. The strategy amplifies the books' visual ability to offer rich symbols for self-fashioning and display.

The highly visual fact of the iBook interface presumes certain technological conditions. High-speed internet access is necessary for multimedia content to flow. So too does the iBook user need certain proprietary hardware and software as well as a lot of computer memory to make the artful book covers appear clearly and instantaneously on the reading device. The cover-facing appearance of books on the iBook's remediated bookshelf indexes tremendous technological changes in digital history over the last twenty years. Recall that graphical browsers didn't emerge until around 1993, so the web at the time of Birkets's lament was text based. Gone are those text- and hypertext-based days of the 1990s. They have been replaced by high-resolution imagery and multimedia content, and the iBook's bookish interface is a result. The now-iconic iBook bookshelf suggests that much has changed in the last few decades in how digital technologies operate and how they mediate our relationship to books. What remains present, however, is the fact that the imagery of the book is a kind of class marker and means of social infrastructure. Long gone are medieval libraries with spines facing inward, but the iBook shelf also presumes certain kinds of class privilege and (digital) literacies for the use of its books.

In the realm of big, digital data and highly visual interfaces, the symbol and vocabulary of the book still reigns. Though e-readers could have developed in multiple ways, they adopted the visual and linguistic semiotics of the codex.[41] Just think of how strange but also strangely familiar is the sound of a digital page turning on a tablet.[42] And, as bookishness demonstrates, books are everywhere in digital culture—as remediated content online, mimicked in the codexical design of laptops and e-readers that open to virtual "pages," and even in bookish accoutrements for digital devices such as laptop covers and cell-phone holders. It is now commonplace to find the presence of the book where it is not actually physically present. The example of the iBook interface demonstrates this fact of contemporary culture and references a central aspect of bookishness: the desire to have books face us even if they are only virtually there.

"To understand books is to understand the act of looking that transpires between us and them."[43] Andrew Piper reminds us that the physical presence of books, their *thereness*, matters to our understanding to them, historically and even today in our contemporary, digital age. "It is this thereness that is both essential for understanding the medium of the book (that books exist as finite objects in the world) and also for reminding us that we cannot think about our electronic future without contending with its ante-cedent, the bookish past."[44] While early book eulogists like Birkets and Carr lamented an idea of losing bookish "depth," what they perhaps were speaking of was actually a particular kind of physical contact: a "thereness" we experience as depth because it's so deep within the constitution of ourselves. What happens when books don't face us anymore, when the mediating interface of the com-puter screen greets us more often than the book's physicality? The iBook interface is one answer. The following chapters explore a vast array of other ways that bookishness allows books to remain part of our digital lives and the objects of our affection.

2

SHELTER

Little solace comes to those
who grieve when thoughts keep
drifting as walls keep shifting
and this great blue world of
ours seems a house of leaves
moments before the wind.

—MARK Z. DANIELEWSKI, *HOUSE OF LEAVES*

Contemporary literature saturates itself, almost obsessively, with books. Bookishness literature turns this obsession into a narrative trope: the figuration of the book as a shelter from the dangerous, digital world. Often without explicitly discussing computers or the internet, bookishness texts allegorically figure books as outposts from the always-on, constant crisis of information overload. They depict books as physical bulwarks against surveillance culture, global capitalism, and terrorism. And they do this *within* books—through allegorical narrative.

I begin with an epigraph from Mark Z. Danielewski's very bookish experimental novel *House of Leaves* (2000), a novel that both manifests and addresses the fragile feeling of books—houses of leaves, in the book's terms—in that early digital moment. This quotation suggests two things. First, that we live in precarious times ("moments before the wind"). Second, implicitly, that book-bound novels (like *House of Leaves* itself) serve as precious sites of refuge, spaces for reflecting on the "thoughts [that] keep drifting." In a world that keeps "shifting" because of ever-changing technologies, bookish readers of *House of Leaves* are left "little solace" when faced with the fact that books (houses of leaves of paper) seem perched on the precipice of obsolescence—"moments before the wind."

Bookishness literature responds to this situation. Whether addressing the tragedy of 9/11 or Silicon Valley's capitalistic sprawl, bookishness narratives depict a world changing so quickly that characters—much like us readers—can't keep up. Books and bookspaces (libraries, reading rooms, and bookstores) appear as places for refuge, restoration, and reconstitution of the self in tumultuous times. As the examples collected in this chapter demonstrate, bookishness narratives process contemporary anxieties *in and through* the image of the book, showing books to be integral to the experience of the digital by offering ways of recovering from and reintegrating into it.

Yet even as these bookishness narratives often figure the book as separate from the digital, they also—though to different degrees and in different ways—reflect the sensibility of bookishness, which, as I have been arguing, comes into being precisely through an interaction with the digital. As such, the visions of shelter they offer—their sense of what it would mean, in fact, to be safe—reflect the interpenetration of digital and material understandings of the real, of nearness, of solidity. And just as both digital and material resources are unevenly distributed among readers, so too are the visions of security they generate and affirm.

REFUGE: *THE KEEP*

Jennifer Egan is perhaps best known for her novel *A Visit from the Goon Squad* (2011), which won the Pulitzer Prize. That novel operates in a mode of bookish nostalgia, particularly as it relates to vinyl records and the changing (that is, digitizing) music industry. Here, however, I turn to an earlier and less-known novel of hers, *The Keep* (2006), to tease out an allegorical trope of bookishness. Egan's *The Keep* does not appear to be particularly bookish in terms of either its content or its form. The novel, to use a bookish term, is a page-turner—a mystery about an enigmatic castle that brings out the inner demons of its visitors. Books aren't its topic, and (unlike *House of Leaves*) it doesn't experiment with page design or typography in any way that would make a reader conscious of the book they are encountering. But even so, *The Keep* has a subtle quality of bookishness that reflects the presence (even omnipresence) of bookishness as an operating force in contemporary literature, even when not overtly on display.

The Keep contains three narrators and three interlocking, nested narratives: (1) Danny, an aging loner who leaves New York City and goes on the lam, visiting his entrepreneurial cousin, Howard, in Eastern Europe; (2) Ray, a prison inmate taking a creative writing class and, in that class, writes a story about Danny and Howard; and (3) Holly, Ray's writing instructor, who falls for him and his story. The embedded narrative—the story within a story within a story— orbits around Howard's plan (remember both Howard and his plan are fictional, even within the world of *The Keep*) to turn a medieval European castle into an upscale hotel for guests seeking to escape their hectic, technologically plugged-in lives. No TVs, phones, or computers will be allowed in this refurbished castle. It will instead serve as a place to reclaim an earlier time, when "*imaginations* were

more active" and when "inner lives were rich and weird."[1] The
rooms of the castle-hotel contain medieval antiques alongside
more recent forms of obsolete technologies: "Danny saw a typewriter and a sewing machine, old ones without plugs, but still. It
gave him a weird impression that the long-ago past was in perfect
shape." The novel is named after the part of a castle wherein, in the
past, "everyone holed up if the castle got invaded. Kind of a last
stand. The stronghold"[2]—which is also how Howard imagines his
hotel, as a stronghold against digital invasion. Howard enlists
his cousin Danny's help in his battle to build a keep, that is, a hotel
and a refuge, to keep out modern technology so that imaginations
can rejuvenate.

In the novel *The Keep* this stronghold is both a building and a
story, and the slippage between the two demonstrates the novel's
vision of books as modes of protection in a digital age. *The Keep* is
metonymically about how literature provides refuge—from prison
(for Danny), an unhappy life (for Holly), networked reality (for the
reader). The bookish part of the narrative operates through metafiction: the storyline about Danny escaping to Europe and con-
fronting his childhood trauma turns out to be a story written by
Ray, the prison inmate. Ray transcends the walls of his jail cell
by writing literature, a skill he learns from Holly. Ray and Holly fall
in love, and their love is entwined with a love of literature.

The narrative pieces are not separate here, and in this way,
Egan's novel marks itself as differently oriented toward the digital
than Ray's story about Howard's fantasy hotel. Ray, in prison,
imagines Howard desiring a "keep" against the digital: a place
where imaginations can be free by virtue of their isolation. But
that is not the vision of Egan's novel, which values the way that
books and the digital work together to create new ideas of authenticity. The stories in Egan's book are interwoven, and so too are
books and digital life. Howard builds the castle for digital refugees;

the novel *The Keep* presents itself as a bookbound literary outpost for imaginations that depends upon the context of the digital for its power.

Egan's novel concludes its bookishness allegory with Holly finding some respite from her life as a single mother and recovering addict with a brief trip to Europe, where she vacations at a hotel named (yes!) "The Keep." Here the narrative takes its most metareflexive turn. The castle-turned-hotel that Ray wrote about in his story for Holly's class now becomes a real place. A card in Holly's hotel room welcomes her in words that Ray's character, Howard, might have written: "The Keep is an electronics- and telecommunications-free environment. Close your eyes, breathe deeply: you can do it."[3]

The novel doesn't end with Holly reading; instead, we see Holly breathing deeply and diving into a swimming pool, and the details of the scene register the omnipresence of the digital and the role of the book in it. The text shifts to first-person narration:

> as I walk to the edge of the pool I'm filled with an old, childish excitement. I wait, letting the snow fall and melt on my hair and face and feet. I let the excitement build until it floods my chest.
>
> I close my eyes and dive in.

But, before she plunges into the watery depths, Holly hears the sound of snow falling and landing on marble. "A trillion invisible clicks."[4] These are the clicks of snow on a hard surface, but they are also the sounds of computer users everywhere. The soundtrack for a woman diving into a swimming pool registers the digital to be part of the everyday, even the natural world. There is no real retreat, nor does there need to be. Instead, embracing a bookishness attitude informed by digital reconfiguration of authenticity and proximity, Egan's novel suggests that immersion—whether in a swimming pool or a bookbound novel—is about harnessing the power and influence of the digital to inspire literature and a love of books.

RECONSTITUTION: *THE ZERO* AND *EXTREMELY LOUD & INCREDIBLY CLOSE*

In Jess Walter's *The Zero*, the force to keep at bay isn't overstimulation; it's global terrorism. Terrorism and digitality, the novel believes, are intertwined, syllogistic threats because contemporary terrorism is dependent upon the digital network. Thus, terrorism registers as primarily a conflict of *media* rather than of politics or ideology—or, put differently, media difference (rather than religion or politics) becomes the primary ideological difference. In this cultural context, the book, specifically its material presence, becomes simultaneously the central metaphor for what terrorism has harmed and a powerful site for reconstitution of self in the wake of cultural trauma.

The novel begins in the aftermath of 9/11. After the towers fall, paper fills the New York City skyline. The novel figures these scraps as birds that "burst into the sky, every bird in creation, angry and agitated, awakened by the same primary thought, erupting in a white feathered cloudburst, anxious and graceful, angling in ever-tightening circles toward the ground, drifting close enough to touch, and then close enough to see that it wasn't a flock of birds at all—it was paper. Burning scraps of paper. All the little birds were paper."[5] Paper here—parallel to the "clicks" in Egan's novel—becomes both a relic and a natural force. From this opening, *The Zero* maintains an obsessive, even fetishistic focus on paper. It suggests that only by saving, organizing, and binding the paper remnants of 9/11 into a book can we begin to recover from the tragedy.

Paper materially permeates *The Zero*; it has also infiltrated the consciousness of Walter's protagonist, Brian Remy. When Remy recalls the tragedy of September 11, he sees paper. It is a signifier and symptom of the trauma. "He remembered smoke and he remembered standing alone while a billion sheets of paper fluttered to the ground.... He remembered walking beneath the long shadows and watching the paper fall as a grumble rose beneath his feet." The novel describes his eye damage, received at Ground Zero, through paperish tropes: "flashes and floaters that danced like scraps of paper blown into the world." Paper is a thing, concept, and symbol, but it is also the object of Remy's quest: a way for Remy to turn trauma into narrative. Remy is a cop and head of the "Documentation department," the fictional bureaucracy of the novel's bookish imaginary, tasked with collecting the paper strewn over New York City after the Twin Towers fell. He works at an airplane hangar "full of people, filing cabinets, and tables of burned and dirty paper."[6] The title and description of the Documentation department registers for *The Zero*'s readers the importance and endurance of paper documents, particularly in a culture of increasing digitization.

The Documentation department is described as a hub of paper waiting to be bound. "As far as Remy could see, these tables were covered with paper—notes, forms, resignations, and retributions, as if the whole world could be conjured up out of the paper it had produced." The language of conjuring, of restoring the ghosts of the past through magic, is aligned with the act of collecting, arranging, and binding paper into books. In the ensuing narrative, Remy attempts to collect and make sense of the paper detritus, to archive the ruins and, in so doing, put to rest the trauma of 9/11. Remy's boss testifies before Congress that the rationale for the Documentation department task force goes beyond cleaning up the streets; it also has an ontological purpose: "*There is nothing so important as recovering the record of our commerce, the proof of our place in the world, of the resilience of our economy, of our jobs, of our lives. If we do not make a fundamental accounting of what was lost, if we do not gather up the paper and put it all back then the forces aligned against us have already won.*"[7] The operating logic displayed here is that if we can collect all of the paper, put it back in order, and bind it into a book—even the paper that did not originally come from books—then everything will be OK. Significantly, books are not what the terrorists attacked, but books—retroactively recuperating the past as "proof of our place in the world"—are what will prove that the terrorists have not won.

There is a media-based logic at work here. If we think back sixty years to Marshall McLuhan's groundbreaking work of media studies *The Gutenberg Galaxy* (1962), we can hear an echo of *The Zero*'s belief in the power of the book medium. McLuhan argued that the invention of print ushered in a modern Western culture that privileged rationality, repetition, and individualism and that, moreover, "our age translates itself back into the oral and auditory modes because of the electronic pressure of simultaneity."[8] He prophesied the emergence of an electric age that would upend the reign of "typographic man." Since contemporary global terrorism relies on electronic infrastructures and networked logics, it's been easy for Western culture—already self-identified with the book as symbol of both individual and cultural expression—to align terrorism's operative force with the digital. Through this logic, in an America embroiled in endless wars against terrorist forces who have weaponized the internet, much literary culture refocuses on the power of the book as a force for good.

Jonathan Safran Foer's *Extremely Loud & Incredibly Close* (2005) offers a different example of how bookishness narratives depict the book as a means of refuge and constitution against contemporary terrorism. *Extremely Loud & Incredibly Close* was published at nearly the same time as Walter's *The Zero*, and like that novel, Foer's protagonist also uses paper as a means of rehabilitation after the trauma of 9/11. Nine-year-old Oskar Schell lost his father in the falling towers, and he records his own crumbling world in a scrapbook titled "Stuff That Happened to Me." His book-based activities are a kind of bibliotherapy. The scrapbook is both a place of refuge from trauma and also a testament to it.

Unlike *The Zero* and *The Keep*, however, *Extremely Loud & Incredibly Close* is a formally inventive novel that engages its book format to present a bookish allegory. This formal experimentation begins before the title page. A black-and-white photograph of a keyhole covers the page, presenting the book as a space to unlock and enter. Upon turning this page, as if peering through the keyhole, the reader encounters another black-and-white photograph, this time of pigeons soaring in the sky. As in *The Zero*, birds introduce the reader to a 9/11 novel that narrates the process of psychological reconstitution through the act of making a book from scraps of paper left behind after the falling towers. The image of the birds is followed by a page containing a blurry photograph of a row of windows, the upper story of a New York City apartment building. Together, the three photographic pages introduce *Extremely Loud & Incredibly Close* as a scrapbook and archive: a magical medium for the conjuring up of lost ghosts (as in the line from Walter's *The Zero* quoted earlier, "as if the whole world could be conjured up out of the paper it had produced").

But Foer's novel does not rest with this idea; in fact, it posits paperlessness as a solution. At the end of *Extremely Loud & Incredibly Close*, Oskar considers whether he should start a new volume of his scrapbook, and the scene solidifies the novel's bookishness. Oskar recalls that he had heard that paper had fueled the burning of the Twin Towers. The idea sparks the following meditation on the possibility of a paperless (that is, digital) world:

I felt in the space between the bed and the wall, and found *Stuff That Happened to Me*. It was completely full. I was going to have to start a new volume soon. I read that it was the paper that kept the towers burning. All of those notepads, and Xeroxes, and printed e-mails, and photographs of kids, and books, and dollar bills in wallets, and documents in files ... all of them were fuel. Maybe if we lived in a paperless society, which lots of scientists say we'll probably live in one day soon, Dad would still be alive. Maybe I shouldn't start a new volume.[9]

Although the reader knows that the jet fuel was the primary cause of the towers' rapid incineration, here Oskar imagines paper as a site of control—and thus imagines that a paperless, digital society might stave off future terrorist threats by withholding the paper "fuel."[10] In the lines that follow, Foer directs the reader's attention to Oskar's paper-filled tome—"I grabbed a flashlight from my backpack and aimed it at the book"[11]—and also to the book we hold in our hands. Foer's book has only one more page of text. Oskar will choose not to start a second volume; insofar as he has traveled from a sense of helplessness to a sense of power, his bibliotherapy was successful (even as his misapprehension tinges his solution, for the more informed reader, with melancholy).

The novel ends by returning to the visual scrapbook style of sequential images with which it began. Foer presents Richard Drew's famous photographs, the Falling Man series, in reverse order, so that the images of an unknown man falling from the World Trade Center tower instead shows him landing safely in an intact building before it burns.[12] Foer rewrites history, and Oskar reconstitutes his traumatized psyche, both through the creation of a book. Thus despite its different relation to the digital, *Extremely Loud & Incredibly Close* shares a logic of bookishness with *The Zero*: both

9/11 novels identify the book as a powerful medium for personal and social recovery in an age of dangerous digital networks.

RECONNECTION: *THE FANTASTIC FLYING BOOKS OF MR. MORRIS LESSMORE*

Adults are not the only readers learning to appreciate books—*through* books—in a digital age. Children's and young adult literature also teach these bookish lessons across a variety of genres and formal methods. *The Fantastic Flying Books of Mr. Morris Lessmore* (2012), by William Joyce and illustrated by Joyce and Joe Bluhm, is a popular and successful picture book that depicts book spaces sheltering battered souls suffering not from terrorism but from Hurricane Katrina.

The Fantastic Flying Books of Mr. Morris Lessmore begins with an illustration of a man sitting in a green chair on his balcony, reading a book in absolute contentment.[13] Stacks of books surround him. The recto page contains the opening text: "Morris Lessmore loved words. / He loved stories. / He loved books." This scene of bookish tranquility quickly dissolves. With a turn of the page, the world is turned upside down, literally. Hurricane Katrina hits, and Morris is thrown up into a tumultuous gray sky along with his books. When the storm passes and another page is turned, Morris is sitting on the ground. His house is upended behind him, and paper is strewn all around. Devastated, he "didn't know what to do or which way to go." So he wanders and encounters a lovely lady drifting in the sky with a bunch of flying books, like helium balloons. She hands him one of the magical books, and it guides him to "an extraordinary building where many books apparently 'nested.'" He makes this enchanted library his new home, a place of refuge from future storms and the source of a new bookish identity. Morris becomes caretaker to the books, a doctor and friend. He "found great satisfaction in caring for the books, / gently fixing those with fragile bindings / and unfolding the dog-eared pages of others."

The house is presented as a shelter for both Lessmore and the books; as for Remy and Oskar, fixing books is for Lessmore both a material and metaphoric act. It's also an allegorical refuge from or complement to the digital spaces that books sometimes share. Sara Tanderup points out that the "the library in *Morris Lessmore* is not presented as a place for mere preservation of the past" but rather as a means for "keeping the tradition alive" for born-digital natives.[14] The magical library and its happy, flying books entice kids to love books, and this lesson is particularly meaningful because readers of *Lessmore* might arrive at the book only after encountering its digital versions. And note that this bookish book *is only one part* of a trans-medial network that comprises *Lessmore*. The narrative began as an animated short film (which won the Academy Award for Best Animated Short Film in 2011) and a year later became an iPad app and picture book. The book's bookishness is thus amplified by other media—"the book 'mimes' the app"[15]—meaning that learning to love books, the pedagogical lesson at the heart of *Lessmore*, depends upon a networked circuit of other media. Loving books in a digital age entails the digital network.

Lessmore's bookish allegory concludes with a didactic lesson. The last page depicts Lessmore sitting contentedly reading a book, and the illustration echoes the book's first page. But here, a pair of hands—the size of a young child's—appear, as if holding the book containing the image. The book takes on a mirror or doubling quality, producing a moment of reflexive recognition that seals the analogy between the young reader and Lessmore, the diegetic book lover. This concluding moment depicts the child reader, whose primary reading medium just might be a digital device rather than a book, seeing herself reflected in the book.[16] "Books have never been just objects of reading," Andrew Piper writes. "To understand books is to understand the act of looking that transpires between us and them."[17] In its narrative and concluding imagery, *Lessmore* teaches the young reader to see her relationship to books as intimate and safe. *Put your hands here on the book, my child, and all will be OK.*

RECOGNITION: *MR. PENUMBRA'S 24-HOUR BOOKSTORE*

Lessmore teaches young readers to recognize the book as a thing to hold close, and Robin Sloane's *Mr. Penumbra's 24-Hour Bookstore* (2012) teaches a similar lesson to adult readers: to see anew the power of the book as a physical, material medium. Its narrative values the book as an emblem for proximity—nearness—rather than simply a conduit for information (that might be processed through other media). Set in the heart of digital capitalism, in San Francisco and Silicon Valley, the novel turns upon a potentially clichéd plot about an independent bookstore dying in the hometown of Google. But the narrative proves surprising. The protagonist, Clay, is a disinterested employee at a twenty-four-hour bookstore. He discovers that his employer does not actually sell books but instead serves as a front for a strange secret society. The members of this secret collective come and go through the bookstore, without interacting with one another; they check out (though this is not a library) ancient tomes containing cryptic numerical grids and later return them. The secret society is called the Unbroken Spine, and its goal is to decipher a hidden message transcribed by the Renaissance bookmaker Aldus Manutius into a book "called CODEX VITAE—book of life,"[18] which supposedly holds the key to eternal life. The novel thus traffics in the ancient idea of the book as sacred object, including the Book of Life in Judaism (into which Jews believe God writes and seals the names of believers during the holy day of Yom Kippur) and subsequent holy books like the Bible and the Qur'an.[19] *Mr. Penumbra's 24-Hour Bookstore* takes up the mantle of the book as sacred object in a narrative whose mystery revolves around a volume that supposedly contains life-giving messages and is worshipped by faithful believers. Set in the twenty-first century, *Mr. Penumbra's 24-Hour Bookstore* reinvigorates the idea of the book as sacred object by presenting it as a thing whose materiality offers the ultimate source of wisdom and power—God-like immortality.

The novel depicts the members of the Unbroken Spine as human computers working to crack Manutius's code and pits them against the übercomputers at Google. Clay's girlfriend is a loyal Google employee and, more than that, a believer in its corporate project; she represents Siva Vaidhyanathan's concern that "our increasing, uncritical faith in and dependence on [Google]" is a new a kind of technophilic religion.[20] She hatches a plan to crack Manutius's code using the company's high-tech scanners, the backbone of the (real-world) Google Books project and then develop an algorithm to decrypt the scanned content. While members of the Unbroken Spine decipher text-based symbols in old tomes, the Google group breaks the spines of codebooks to scan them in and uses a machine to read them. But both groups—those who do and those who don't crack the spines of the books—fail to crack the code. It is Clay who wins the race to decrypt the secret message.

Clay solves the puzzle of Manutius's text by doing something so obvious, unsophisticated, and untechnological that it had been overlooked by seekers for centuries. He looks *at* the book. While the Google team and the Unbroken Spine demonstrate the similarity between historic and digital cultures by remaining focused on decrypting textual content—that is, reading for the hidden message—Clay reads the object itself. He explains his discovery: Aldus Manutius died and "entrusted Gerritszoon with the key to his encrypted history." "Gerritszoon" names not a person (or just a person) but also a font. While the other readers in this novel assume "Gerritszoon" is code for something else, Clay looks at the actual Gerritszoon type. He surveys the Gerritszoon punches used to shape the formation of moveable type and fonts in early printing processes. In so doing, he recognizes that there, on the thing itself, the physical object used to make words, are "tiny notches" that look like "the teeth of a key." The notches are what need to be counted and decoded, *not* the words in print. The notches are the key to the puzzle that allow the words of the message to be read. The type—the actual, material elements used to produce letters on the page in a printed book—allow Clay to interpret this novel's central mystery. "Nobody in the fellowship's five-hundred-year history thought to look this closely. Neither did any of Google's code-breakers. We were looking at digitized text in a different typeface entirely. We were looking at the sequence, not the shape."[21] Clay solves the puzzle by paying attention to the materiality of the book as medium. He practices media-specific analysis and adopts a McLuhanesque understanding that the medium *is* the message.[22] Like the lesson imparted at the end of *Lessmore*, *Mr. Penumbra's 24-Hour Bookstore* also teaches us to look *at*, not just into or through, the media we use.

Learning to recognize the specificities of media has never been so important or so challenging than in our contemporary digital age. The more that Google and other corporations render proprietary their digital software, the more that technological processes become distributed through cloud computing rather than located on specific machines, and the more that layers of user-friendly programming platforms enable creation without knowledge of operation, the less we understand about how the media we use operates, both for us and *on* us. In this way, the suspicion of the digital is more than just a knee-jerk aversion to change. Further, because political and personal or even outright prejudiced biases are often imparted into digital code and programs, the operations of these digital media demand critical analysis.[23] The fact that books are physical, stable, and discrete objects might render them easier to know than digital technologies, but, as *Mr. Penumbra's 24-Hour Bookstore* illustrates, that doesn't mean we know them well. The novel reminds us that we need to understand all the media we use, including the book. Moreover, concern with digitality just might promote our learning about books.

SHELTER FOR WHOM? THE PRIVILEGE OF BOOKISHNESS

The depiction of the book as a site of refuge and shelter from the digital and its related threats raises the question: shelter for whom? Who desires escape, and who gets to retreat from the digital age and its increasingly complicated technologies? In other words, what privilege is presumed by bookishness?[24]

Books have long served as symbols of class—literacy and learning, power and wealth. Being bookish, attaining a nearness to books, depends upon an ability to possess or access books (either money to purchase and/or knowledge about how to borrow) and, thus, a certain kind of privilege. This was especially true when books were expensive and nearness to them turned the book into a referent of social status. So what does it mean that most of the authors examined in this chapter about allegories of bookishness are white men? (Egan is the only female.) Across the board, white male authors predominate allegorical narratives of bookishness, and within those novels, white men (Mr. Lessmore, Mr. Penumbra) predominate as bookish emblems. This fact offers not only a necessary frame for bookishness literature but also a useful point of comparison to an earlier literary period: postmodernism.

Of the many things we might say about postmodern literature, let me focus on one relevant question: its relation to technology. In *The Anxiety of Obsolescence: The American Novel in the Age of Television*, Kathleen Fitzpatrick argues that postmodern literature (roughly from the 1960s through the 1980s) centered around fears of television and mass culture; moreover, these fears served a strategic purpose for white male writers. The novel, Fitzpatrick argues, was "not dying but democratizing," and novelists responded by translating fears of multiculturalism and feminism into narratives of technophobia. In so doing, they created a shared sensibility and coterie readership around a defensiveness to mass media: "the cachet of marginality serves to create a protected space within which the novel can continue as an art by restricting itself to those few readers equipped to appreciate it."[25] Something similar might be at work in bookishness.

Though bookishness is not solely a highbrow art form, as the novels in this chapter demonstrate, it does traffic in translating social fears into aesthetic practices and allegorical tropes (for instance, translating the complex history of conflict and antagonism between the United States and al-Qaeda into a conflict about the digital). Much has transpired between the 1980s and today, both culturally and technologically, but the anxiety of obsolescence remains alive and well. We saw it at work in the slogan of Donald Trump's presidential campaign "Make America Great Again" and understand that only some share nostalgia for an imagined American past. The same might be true of a nostalgia for a bookish past. The anxiety of too much digital—always-on-ness (Egan's *The Keep*), global terrorism (Walter's *The Zero* and Foer's *Extremely Loud & Incredibly Close*), absolute faith in digital corporations (Sloane's

Mr. Penumbra's 24-Hour Bookstore)—is a sign of the times. But it is certainly also a sign of certain people's experience of the times or, perhaps, a sign that will be read differently by different people.

The structural format of the book chafes against digital networks and the experience of anxiety that they promote for those (privileged enough to live) connected to them. "The book is a slow form of exchange," Carla Hesse writes.[26] The literary scholar Christina Lupton agrees: "there's a slowing down, a repetition, a promise, associated with book reading that pulls back on the logic of accumulation and acceleration, and the measurement of time."[27] That is why bookishness coincides with other movements seeking to stave off the fast-paced, networked exchange of digital capitalism. When email and digital devices enable work to be done on a beach as well as in an office, workers have little ability to escape labor; alternatively, they willingly participate in exploitative "playbor" culture.[28] The recent surge of "slow" movements (slow food, slow scholarship, etc.) attests to desires to resist the neoliberal productivity regime.[29]

Yet, as ubiquitous as these desires might be, the ability to slow down and seek shelter in a book might be a position of privilege (just as the ability to have a fast, functional phone and unlimited data plan certainly is, even as it's an exploitable privilege). Consider how elementary school students in American public schools do much of their learning on digital tablets, yet elite private schools in Silicon Valley—those schools that educate the children of the digerati who make and sell digital technoculture—have adopted low-tech educational practices.[30] This fact should remind us that our relationship to technology is never just a binary of have and have not but is about how we choose to understand these tools—as detriments to imagination (like Howard in *The Keep*) or as "dream machines" that stimulate imagination (à la Ted Nelson's early vision of the computer).[31] Bookishness raises questions about the relationship between digital and books but also about how these media are associated with and informed by class and privilege.

As the examples from this chapter demonstrate, bookishness narratives often operate subtly, in ways that prompt readers to pause, reflect, and reread in order to understand them. These texts demonstrate how literature retains a vital role as a space for cultural critique and comprehension, especially in our complex, networked times. Bookishness literature charts a culture adjusting to digital life by offering the book itself as a vehicle—often exaggerated in its powers but also resonant in its potential—for recovery and recalibration.

3

THING

A book is a thing. A dictionary can describe that thing—"A portable volume consisting of a series of written, printed, or illustrated pages bound together for ease of reading" is how the *Oxford English Dictionary* defines it—but not the force of its thingness. Bookishness situates the thingness, the artifactuality, of books in cultural time—so we can read the emotional force of that thingness as a product of the now.

Historically, the book has run the gamut from sacred to profane thing. The codex helped spread Christianity, and the book became the Book—the sacred object for holding and knowing the word of God.[1] "To believe in the book and believe in God gradually became synonymous."[2] Over time, this syllogism enabled the book to become a meaningful object regardless of the content it contained. But, books have also been used as storage devices, decoration, coasters, souvenirs, and trash. Watch a toddler play with one for a few minutes and you'll see the book used as a teething tool, an airplane, a building block, and maybe even something to open and peruse. Books mean differently to different people, and even to the same person at different times. The book may be a thing, but it is never only one thing. Yet the thingly aspect of the book matters, especially in a digital age.

"To matter is not only to be of importance, to signify, to mean, but also to claim a certain physical space, to have a particular presence, to be uniquely embodied."[3] As an academic and avid reader, I see how my particular social context shapes what feels real about books to me, but I also feel that realness deep in my bones, underneath the point of criticism. During a recent move, my books—the things that have followed me back and forth across the country multiple times, the things that have been given to me by loved ones, the things in which I have written annotations that attest to my intellectual and emotional development—sat in the garage, stacked in boxes, waiting. After a week or so, I felt a sense of emptiness and lack. I missed seeing my books when I entered my home. I needed them for comfort and sometimes for consultation. I felt unmoored without the presence of those things, those books. This personal feeling, I know, isn't just mine: it's a part of the lingering mythos of the book's sacred power. The writer Anne Fadiman nicely captures the intensity of this feeling, speaking in a collective voice that speaks to books' thingness as a means of cultural formation: "Books wrote our life story, and as they accumulated on our shelves . . . they became chapters in it themselves."[4]

The thingness of books, in this world, allows a display of a person's learning, aspirations, and attachments—and so books are also a source of anxiety. This is especially true for an academic. As a professional reader, books can be nasty things. They tease, taunt, and fester. Books I have not yet read pile up into stacks on my desk, physical reminders of my lack of time and knowledge and of my unfulfilled ambitions. In this case, it is their physical presence—not the content they contain (as I have not yet encountered it)—that matters. Yet I want books around and want to feel all the feelings of having them near, for this interchange of attachments is part of how I recognize myself.

Andrew Piper describes the physical presence of the book as its main characteristic: "That is what they are by definition: there." And this "thereness" "is both essential for understanding the medium of the book (that books exist as finite objects in the world) and also for reminding us that we cannot think about our electronic future without contending with its antecedent, the bookish past."[5] The book's thingness—or thereness—has become more desirable in the age of digitization, e-readers, and cloud-based storage libraries. Over the last millennium, the book's *thereness* allowed us to build bookish identities around our *nearness* to it. In a digital age, as the experience of nearness shifts—am I nearer to the person across the country whose face I can see on my screen or the person living next to me behind a closed door?—we find new ways of holding onto and using the *thereness* of the book as thing. Bookishness explores and demonstrates how we do so.

Bookishness, as such, enacts the idea of the fetish—as it was developed from eighteenth-century European colonialists through to Karl Marx (before Freud shifted it into a sexual perversion associated with lack). Fetish is about animating the inanimate by projecting human desire onto the nonhuman. This power of the fetishized object can be religious or mystical (the view of seventeenth-century white Europeans observing the practices of African cultures), capitalistic (in Marx's critique of capitalism and the idea of commodity fetishism), or psychological (in Freud's theory of masculine identity formation). The concept of fetishism has a long history, one that crosses diverse philosophical movements and historical moments, but what remains consistent in the concept of the fetish as it moves from "the cross-cultural spaces of the coast of West Africa during the sixteenth and seventeenth centuries"[6] to Marx's nineteenth-century industrial London to Freud's Vienna at the end of the nineteenth century is that the fetish is always, at its core, about the relationship between humans and things.[7] In his extended study of the fetish concept, William Pietz comes to the conclusion that "the first characteristic to be identified as essential to the notion of the fetish is that of the fetish object's irreducible materiality."[8] Fetishism is about thingness. So when digitization threatens the physicality of books, we see a cultural response: to fetishize the book object.[9]

These intensities and erotics flow in and out of the diverse range of texts this chapter examines—texts that, in different ways, show how books remain there, as things that matter, in a digital age. My examples demonstrate how bookishness presents the book object as a site for the projection of feelings about the changing role of books, and objects more generally. I begin with what I call "it-texts," contemporary literature that adapts an older genre—the "it-narrative"—to depict the book as the central character whose circulation illuminates the changing landscape of the contemporary literary. I then move beyond it-texts and actual books to consider how bookishness turns the book into a fetish object for the digital age—by examining, for example, an exemplary work from the trending genre of short, stop-motion films that use the internet as a distribution platform for making the inanimate book seem to come to life. I conclude by returning to book-based literature, to a particularly unique bookish object that presents the book as a souvenir in and for a culture learning to love anew tangible objects in the wake of digitalization. Collectively, these examples invite us to appreciate the book as a thing—and the importance of things more generally—and to consider why and how its presence matters now.

BOOKISH IT-TEXTS

Bookishness illuminates the value of the book as object in narratives that depict the book as a character, a thing that moves and acts rather than just as a medium to be acted upon. Such narratives update an earlier literary genre, the "it-narrative" of eighteenth- and nineteenth-century Britain. They do so in ways that teach contemporary readers to understand the role of the book as thing and specifically a commodity within a changing world and marketplace.

"During a period of particularly intense social reorganization between 1750 and 1780," Nicolas Hudson explains, "novels narrated from the point of view of nonhuman and inanimate objects pullulated through the bookstalls."[10] With such titles as *Chrysal; or, The Adventures of a Guinea* (1760), *Adventures of a Black Coat* (1760), *Adventures of a Cork-Screw* (1775), and *Adventures of a Hackney Coach* (1781), it-narratives followed small and seemingly insignificant objects as they traveled through society. By focusing on these objects as they moved, readers learned about the emerging and changing structures of industrial capitalism as well as the resulting effects on social class structures.

It-narratives of the nineteenth century shifted their focus to a particular object: the book. "Whereas eighteenth-century it-narrative taught readers the rules governing cash and credit in a commercial society," Leah Price explains, the it-narratives of the nineteenth century "take on a narrower topic: how one very particular kind of consumer good—books—should be bought, sold, borrowed, disposed of."[11] New technologies of industrial production, including the invention of wood pulp and thus cheaper paper, rendered books less precious and more common. As a result, a book was no longer a thing that, by virtue of its market value, might also accrue the sentimental value that comes from the financial necessity of being held on to and passed down. It could now be given away, traded, sold, or otherwise discarded. What might the emotional force of the book as thing become in this new context? As book production, literacy rates, and the middle class developed, nineteenth-century it-narratives adapted to depict and explore this new marketplace and society. Bookish it-narratives inducted bourgeois readers and book buyers into an emerging social network built upon attachments to, and around, books.

Something similar is at work in twenty-first-century bookishness. Contemporary "it-texts"—as I call them to differentiate them from the traditional it-narrative genre—present the book not as the narrator, as in earlier it-narratives, but as a charismatic object that propels action and commands the narrative's plot to develop around it. These works depict books exerting power over humans. They suggest and compel an object-oriented perspective—a way of rethinking traditional distinctions (and hierarchical values) between animate and inanimate, human and nonhuman. The emergence of such it-texts reflects recent critical movements toward which they are particularly attuned, including new materialism, object-oriented ontology, and other critiques of anthropocentrism that reevaluate the role of inanimate actors in our world.[12] Contemporary it-texts follow the lead of their ancestors to narrate a changing situation for books-as-commodities in a new (digital, global, networked) phase of industrial capitalism. These bookish texts follow the book object as it circulates, illuminating the digital and social networks through which bookish culture now emerges.

It-texts illuminate the complex networks that support our attachments to books and to the literary more generally—and thus they help us see networks, often understood to be digital, as not antithetical to bookish ways of being. These texts do so by building and revealing social networks around the book object as hub. They teach us to understand the book via a networked perspective and, accordingly, to understand the digital network via the book object. Such lessons are important because we live in an age of digital networks supported and informed by the internet.

"Networks are not merely a novel object of study; they also alter the very categories through which we think and know."[13] Bookishness it-texts foreground the importance of adopting a networked perspective in order to understand contemporary culture and the role of books within it.

THE HOUSE OF PAPER

My first example of a bookishness it-text is a lovely little book about books: *The House of Paper* (2005) by the Argentine writer Carlos María Domínguez. This slim, hundred-page volume contains a short but deceptively complex story, interlaced with small, fanciful illustrations by Peter Sís. A bibliophile's dream-turned-nightmare, the novel depicts books possessing great power to affect the people around them. Written almost in the mode of magical realism, this short fictional parable also comments on the larger, nonfictional world. It begins, "Books change people's destinies." The text continues, expanding upon this claim: "Some have read *The Tiger of Malaysia* and become professors of literature in remote universities. *Demian* converted tens of thousands of young men to Eastern philosophy, Hemingway made sportsmen of them, Alexandre Dumas complicated the lives of thousands of women, quite a few of whom were saved from suicide." The novel suggests that books not only act upon their readers through their textual content but also through their physical presence. The narrator's German grandmother, who undoubtedly knows at first hand from Nazi Germany that a book can condemn its owner, repeats the refrain "'books are dangerous.'"[14]

The House of Paper's story spools out from a particularly mysterious book object that arrives at our narrator's door via international parcel service after the intended recipient of the package, our narrator's colleague Bluma Lennon, was hit by a car while reading a book. (Yes, we learn quite quickly that books are indeed dangerous.) Our narrator has taken over this dead colleague's position in the Department of Hispanic Studies at Cambridge University and inherits the package. It is covered with Uruguayan stamps and contains a paperback copy of Joseph Conrad's *The Shadow-Line*. The book is a strange thing, marked by "a filthy crust on its front and back covers" and "a film of cement particles on the page edges." It is a singular and haunting object: "no other book has affected me so much as that paperback, whose damp, warped pages seemed to be calling out to me." It is not Conrad's story that proves so compelling; the narrator does not even attempt to read the novel, let alone open the book. Rather, it is the book-object itself that so "upset the balance of the room."[15]

This book emerges as the central character in *The House of Paper*, and the "it" at the center of this bookish it-text is truly an *it*, a monstrous thing. It is described as a living object, a character that "deserved to be returned to whoever had sent it."[16] The descriptor "deserved" tells us about the character of the book: it is an enlivened thing that coerces certain actions. Just as Bluma's book of Dickinson poems absorbed her so completely that she was hit by a car, and, in so doing, pulled our narrator into Bluma's social web (and her book's network), so too does this strange copy of Conrad's *The Shadow-Line* exert a socializing force. As the book seems to demand, the narrator travels to South America to trace the story behind this compelling artifact and return it to its sender.

In Buenos Aires, our narrator learns the story of the book's past movements: when a brilliant book collector loses himself to the madness of bibliophilia, he begins talking to his books and, later, significantly, sleeping with them: "twenty or so books carefully laid out in such a way that they reproduced the mass and outline of a human body." The books, as physical objects, take on an intimate connection to him. He eventually disappears, bringing his vast and expensive book collection with him. He buys a plot of land by the sea and builds a house made completely out of books. He "turn[s] his books into bricks." The books are no longer media for reading or commodities on the marketplace but now strictly serve physical purposes as bricks. "All he worried about was their size, their thickness, how resistant their covers might be to lime, cement and sand." The narrator, fascinated by the story of this reader-collector-contractor, journeys to the possibly apocryphal spot to see for himself the house made out of books. There he finds that "the books were there, they were still there," just "in their tomb of sand."[17] The books are depicted as living, dying, and decomposing things—corpses on the shore, where inanimate and animate objects (the books, their deranged collector, and other random sea crea-tures) together waste away on a forgotten beach. This amazing lit-tle bookish it-text tells the tale of the survival of a book—the book that a mad collector sent to his lover, Bluma, before succumbing to madness—and presents an allegory about the survival of books in a digital age. *The House of Paper* shows books to be things that connect people into networks of relationships across oceans, continents, and time, and they do so by making us relish in their bookishness.

BETWEEN PAGE AND SCREEN

Digital social networks enable their users to feel known, to feel con-nected and seen. Sometimes a bookishness it-text does this too. It makes its reader feel as if she is being addressed directly. So con-sider this: you, not just anyone, but you, hold in your hands a little red book. It is a lovely thing: a thin seven-inch square made of thick cardstock whose textured cover appears woven because of the finely printed diagonal lines repeating, in very small print, its title:

Between Page and Screen.[18] But when you open its covers, you realize immediately that this book is not for you, after all.[19] The ink printed on the stark white page displays a strange image: a black square. The square is printed at the center of the page, and it contains a white geometric pattern. That's it. There's no text to read. Just this shape. Variations of these black-and-white images appear at the center of each page in the little book. These patterns are QR (quick response) codes, and they signify the opportunity for digital information to be scanned and decoded by a digital reader. So it's only when you hold the book up to the webcam on your computer—yes, yours—and when the computer is connected to the internet (and to a specific page, www.betweenpageandscreen.com) that a digital connection is made and something magical happens: a projection of three-dimensional text appears between page and screen.

Amaranth Borsuk and Brad Bouse's *Between Page and Screen* (2012) is a work of augmented-reality (AR) literature that operates through computational processes and acts of translation across a

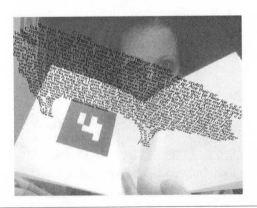

FIGURE 3.1 The projection of three-dimensional text appears between page and screen in Amaranth Borsuk and Brad Bouse's *Between Page and Screen* (2012). Photograph by Brad Bouse.

Source: Permission to use image granted by artists.

network of animate and inanimate actors—including the computer, the webcam, an internet connection, programming code, software, the human reader, and the book. When these entities—one of whom is *you*—work together, they produce a literary performance that highlights simultaneously the thingness of the book and also the book's capacity to participate in a digital circuit.

Between Page and Screen is also an it-text narrative whose central characters, P and S, are anthropomorphic representations of page and screen. These characters conduct an epistolary correspondence— oscillating between flirtatious and fighting—that happens across and between the interfaces of the reader's page and screen. While they do so, the augmented aspect of the work challenges deeply held beliefs about how we read books. The work stages a scene of reading very different than the traditional image we have inherited over the centuries.[20]

The scene of the silent, individual reader staring deep into an open book is a known and poignant symbol of interiority and selfhood. We have learned to associate this image with privacy, lei- sure time, and class. *Between Page and Screen* challenges and compli- cates traditional postures of reading and the meanings associated with them. We do not stare into this book and dive toward the deep- est parts of its spine. You read by gazing *not* at the actual pages but at their reflection onscreen. You look to your computer screen and see your face alongside or occluded by the book and the text pro- jecting out from its open pages. The book is a surface *not* for the projection of the human self into the text but for the webcam to scan and read. And we read not by applying a skill we've learned elsewhere but by responding to specifically *this* book and how it interacts with the camera to teach us how to find the angles that enable the projection of text and thus make meaning.

Between Page and Screen updates the it-text genre by anthropo- morphizing objects (page and screen) into the characters P and S and by using the actual objects they reference to teach lessons about how to handle books. These lessons are very different from those of traditional nineteenth-century it-narratives. Here the focus is less on books as commodities whose place in culture has changed and more on how the practices and participants of reading have changed. *Between Page and Screen* dispels the assumption that humans are the only readers of literature, an ideology of the page and of anthropocentrism that has been long associated with codexical media. This AR it-text prompts us to recognize digital code *as* text and the computer as the reader of it. For the human reader, to see the QR codes in the pages of the book *Between Page and Screen* is to encounter a language one cannot read—or, to use the other literary genre involved in this work, an epistolary correspondence that one cannot decode. These signs are addressed *not* to you, the human reader, but to the machine. This digital text tells the camera what to look for, which data files to retrieve, and how to process them. Like RFID tags and other forms of digitally encoded inscription, this text is intended for machines and for activities that we might not even consider to be reading.

While the human reader ponders the linguistic twists and turns of the etymological wordplay in the epistolary communication between P and S, other acts of reading and translation are taking place with the digital, machinic actors.[21] Readers of *Between Page and Screen* come to understand the augmented technological circuit of page, screen, book, webcam, internet, etc. as a new stage— both a temporal and physical location—in the history of the book.[22] This it-text thus teaches readers to recognize the book—this book, specifically, but also perhaps the book more generally—as an object that can (and often does) operate within a transmedial circuit. We see the book not as separate from the digital or in a relationship of antagonism to it but, instead, as integral to it.

FETISH OBJECTS AND SOUVENIRS

Stop-Motion Bookishness: The Joy of Books

A hand turns a key and locks the door as night falls on the front window of a small independent bookstore. The camera holds fast to the books displayed on stands facing the street. A moment passes in stillness. Then one of the books rotates, pivoting its cover toward the sounds of footsteps disappearing down the sidewalk. Two-toned music instills anticipation as the camera moves inside the bookstore, panning across the dark interior. Then, magic. A book slides out of its place on the shelf, and then another, poking out from the stacks to make sure that the coast is clear. One of the books, suggestively, is a *Masters of Cinema* volume with Victor Van Dort on its cover and dedicated to Tim Burton, a pioneer in stop-motion filmmaking, the art form making these inanimate objects move. More notes enrich the musical score, then percussion takes over. The camera pans over a counter covered with books laid flat. One book's cover flutters open, as if waking from a long slumber. Then the bookstore comes to life. The lights turn on, the music quickens, and all of the books start to move, jumping into a choreographed dance—a bookish Busby Berkeley dream. The books play on the shelves, arranging and rearranging their spines in a shifting kaleidoscope of color.[23] Little journals, pens, and other bookstore oddities perform geometric arrangements on nearby stands. This is *The Joy of Books* (2012), a stop-motion film by Sean and Lisa Ohlenkamp.[24]

The film went viral online, gaining 2.5 million views in its first month and much attention in the blogosphere (a then-thriving part of internet production). One response from a blogger at *Mashable* articulates the poetic paradox at the heart of the film: "Watching this video made me think about the importance of old-fashioned books, still playing a role even in my techno-environment that's been almost taken over by digital content."²⁵ *The Joy of Books* uses the new media of the internet as distribution platform to make its viewer "think about the importance of old-fashioned books." In its employment of new modes of digitality to literally animate the nondigital book object and stimulate desire ("joy") for it, the video is absolute bookishness.

The Joy of Books ends in the wee hours of the morning. The sun begins to rise, and the books fall back into their places on the shelves. The magic of the night gives way to stasis and normalcy. In the final moments of the film, the camera zooms in on a particular section of a bookshelf, where a single hardcover book stands out from its surroundings. Framed by colorful spines on the shelves around it, this book alone faces forward and wears a stark gray cover. Its position and appearance distinguish it, and for good reason. On its cover, a white rectangle contains the following claim: "There's Nothing Quite Like a Real Book."

The book's title is a statement and an argument. It suggests that this thing known as "a real book" is in some kind of imminent danger; why else the need for a reminder that there's nothing like it? Before settling into stillness, to resume the role of object and commodity on the bookstore shelf, this singular book—with its argument about "a real book"—flutters its cover twice. The gesture suggests the book having the last laugh before the film ends and also registers a bit flirtatiously, as if it is opening its cover to let out, ever so briefly, a promiscuous page. The nexus of fear, joy, and desire at the heart of this film and expressed in this moment invites consideration. What is "a real book," and why should we care? What is so special about it?

The answers become clear when we zoom out from this final shot to situate *The Joy of Books* in a larger constellation of similar works dedicated to proclaiming the power of the book object in a

FIGURE 3.2 Screenshot of final shot of *The Joy of Books* (2012), a bookish stop-motion film by Sean Ohlenkamp and Lisa Ohlenkamp.

digital age and, importantly, via the internet. *The Joy of Books* is exemplary of a genre of short (nearly all are under three minutes) stop-motion films that exist online and exemplify bookishness. Taken together, these films form a sample set evidentiary of a larger artistic movement that uses a mode of old-fashioned film-making to express appreciation of the book object in the digital age. Other examples include *Going West* (2009), a beautiful stop-motion movie created by Andersen M Studio for the New Zealand Book Council that uses around three thousand still images to turn an excerpt from Maurice Gee's novel *Going West* (1992) into a physical, artifactual, and animated landscape.[26] The camera zooms in on pages that fill the frame and expand to become a paper landscape made to resemble the setting of the story. A voiceover narrates, and the story comes to life. A train track, trees, and grass—all cut carefully from paper—appear on the surface of the page and demonstrate how that page is a stage upon which the story takes shape, physically: the novel's story comes to the reader not through printed words on the page but instead is delivered through the three-dimensional movement of cut paper, the medium of the page.

This Is Where We Live (2008), released by Apt Studio and Asylum Films in the United Kingdom, on the other hand, uses both paper and words to tell its story—although in this film, the line between book as object and book as text blurs.[27] The film uses stop-motion techniques to create a city scene made from books. The camera pans at street view as people made from paper walk along avenues and through districts composed of book covers, spines, and torn-out pages. A flock of paper birds soar above trees cut from paper. They fly across a building made up of a stack of Michael Chabon's *Kavalier and Clay*—and both the fact that the building is composed of books and also that it is *this* particular book matter to the viewer's ability to read, or interpret, this visual story.

Or consider the longer (nearly six minutes) and more narrative-based film by the director Spike Jonze and Olympia Le-Tan, an artist who uses felt to create handbags intricately decorated with beloved book covers, *Mourir auprès de toi* (*To Die by Your Side*) (2011).[28] Like *The Joy of Books*, this stop-motion movie is set inside a bookstore after dark; in this case, the locale is the world-famous Shakespeare and Company in Paris. The film presents a love story between book-ish characters. A skeleton made from felt extracts himself from the stitching attaching him to the cover of *Macbeth* so that he can walk over to Mina Harker, who lies seductively in bed on the cover of *Dracula*. She motions suggestively for him to join her, and thus begins a dark, bookish love story that moves between book covers and across bookshelves in an artful animation about the animated life of books.

But why stop-motion, which is a somewhat antiquated technique for producing movies in the digital age? Stop-motion creates its magic by photographing an object in a series of still shots that, when sped up and run through the projector, depicts the object moving independently, as if alive. The term "stop-motion" refers to stopping the film in order to change something on set so that when filming resumes, the object appears to have moved. Early on, stop-motion was a way to generate special effects—the 1895 film *The Execution of Mary, Queen of Scots*, for instance, used stop-motion in a decapitation scene wherein a dummy was substituted for the live actor playing Mary.[29] *The Humpty Dumpty Circus* (1898) is widely noted as the first stop-motion commercial film; in it, wooden circus toys come to life.

In the twenty-first century, digital technologies and techniques have largely replaced film, cameras, and projection devices. Yet stop-motion not only remains a technique in the cinematic toolbox; it has experienced a renaissance of late. This resurgence for the old mode is in large part thanks to the work of Tim Burton, who is referenced in the homage at the beginning of *The Joy of Books*.[30] The fact that stop-motion filmmaking flourishes today—in the age of computer-generated imagery (CGI) and vector-based animation software, wherein there is no need for still photography or celluloid film—is poignant and paradoxical. The medial shift from books to e-readers and from film to CGI inspires aesthetic acts of nostalgia and defiance, such as the use of predigital modes of animation to express appreciation for the book.

The stop-motion technique effaces the many minute acts that manipulate the object (for example, moving it between cinematic takes), enabling the inanimate to appear animated—and in so doing, it makes specific use of the fetish. Fetishism is not just about loss but also, of course, about desire. The title *The Joy of Books* echoes the famous book *The Joy of Sex* (1972), which used the book medium as a means of making the most private and intimate of acts and desires public, sharable, socially legitimate, and codexical. What does it mean to shift from a book that famously depicts sexual encounters with simple line drawings to a film that brings to life books in suggestively erotic ways? In *The Joy of Books*, after the bookstore's door is closed and locked, the camera allows a voyeuristic experience: secret entry into the hidden life of things. We enter in darkness and spy on books doing what we humans don't get to see them do during the light of day. This otherworldly, after-hours life is sexy and fun, full of flirtatious dancing (a Fred Astaire book dances with one with Ginger Rogers on its cover) and "joy." *The Joy of Books* reflects and also promotes desire for books.

The film is also an advertisement for small, independent bookstores, which have been under threat of closure from the marketshare clout of megacorporations (like Amazon.com) and increasing prevalence of digitized content (like Google Books). Five seconds into the film, *The Joy of Books* identifies the location of this magical bookstore as Type Books, in Toronto, Ontario. In the paratextual content on the YouTube page hosting the film, the sole sentence contained in the description box (just under the name of the author and the date published and just before the contact address for Type Books and the list of credits) is: "Everything you see here can be purchased at Type Books."[31] Besides marketing a specific bookstore, the film also promotes the idea that bookstores contain magical, sacred things: books.

This bookish film about books and bookstores is only made accessible via the power of the internet and video-sharing social media platforms like Youtube.com and Vimeo. Users tweet and embed links to the video *The Joy of Books*, expanding the metatags used to reference the film and thus enabling vintage stop-motion to circulate through the tributaries of the digital social network.[32] Its viral success makes evident that, despite the film's concluding message (that a real book is a hardback purchased at a brick-and-mortar, independent bookstore), the digital network is not antithetical to but in fact a thriving location for the contemporary literary and the bookish.[33]

The final frame of *The Joy of Books* depicts "a real book" as a hardcover in an independent bookstore and as a novel. We know that it is a novel, given its proximate relationship on the shelf to the books surrounding it. It is no surprise that the concept of a "real book"— with "real" signifying nostalgic value in the age of digital, virtual, downloadable, and leased data—is identified not as a textbook, a travel guide, or something else, but as a novel. The book = novel equation does a lot of work in the cultural imagination, much like the print-versus-digital dichotomy, even though neither are neat and true distinctions. The alignment of a medial format (codex), a genre (novel), and a value (good) in the stop-motion film elides and ironically comments upon a truism of contemporary literary culture: the literary—and, indeed, the book—depends upon the digital.[34] *The Joy of Books* demonstrates how the book object acquires new valences as a thing and how bookishness supports its emergence as the fetish object par excellence for the digital age.

Book as Souvenir: Important Artifacts and Personal Property from the Collection of Lenore Doolan and Harold Morris, Including Books, Street Fashion, and Jewelry

The Joy of Books lauds the emotional, almost erotic value of the literary by attaching that experience to one kind of object—the real book—and to one kind of consumer experience—the independent bookstore; the film suggests that the magic bookstore offering bookish intimacy is a refuge from digital capitalism. Leanne Shapton's *Important Artifacts and Personal Property from the Collection of Lenore*

Doolan and Harold Morris, Including Books, Street Fashion, and Jewelry (2009) differently navigates the intersections of emotion and consumption in a book about things. A graphic novella that tells the story of a budding-to-broken relationship between two young writers in New York City, the narrative appears in an explicitly consumeristic form: an auction catalog. The conceit is that an auction house (Strachan & Quinn Auctioneers) is selling off items once owned by Lenore Doolan and Harold Morris: a Tiffany key ring, a silver-plated cup, a handwritten letter, a newspaper clipping, three pairs of women's shoes, etc. Photographs of these objects and the captions describing them provide the only information available on the couple. There is no other narrative text. The book narrates the story of a human relationship *through* inanimate objects, specifically through the curation and presentation of these artifacts into a book that is mimicking the form of another kind of book. The reader—framed by the book as a potential buyer—pieces together the story of this couple by considering what they left behind. *Important Artifacts and Personal Property from the Collection of Lenore Doolan and Harold Morris, Including Books, Street Fashion, and Jewelry* is an archive and souvenir of a relationship and also, I argue, a souvenir of books and analog culture.

The novel begins with two photographs, one of a woman and one of a man, presented side by side in the top section of the page. Lot 1001: "A photograph of Lenore Doolan, age 26. An original color print of Doolan at her desk at the *New York Times*, 2002. Taken by Adam Bainbridge, a coworker. 4 × 6 in. $10–20." Lot 1002: A passport photograph of Harold Morris, age 39. An original print of Morris, taken in 2002 prior to a photography assignment in the Philippines, 2 x 2 in. $10–20."[35]

Reading left to right, top to bottom, the reader infers from the catalog copy that Harold and Lenore were coworkers at the *New York Times*. Below these images are two more: an invitation to a Halloween party (Lot 1003) and a group of photographs of Lenore

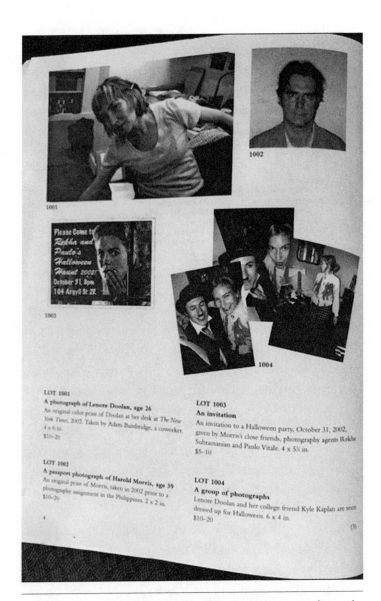

LOT 1001
A photograph of Lenore Doolan, age 26
An original color print of Doolan at her desk at *The New York Times*, 2002. Taken by Adam Bainbridge, a coworker. 4 x 6 in.
$10–20

LOT 1002
A passport photograph of Harold Morris, age 39
An original print of Morris, taken in 2002 prior to a photography assignment in the Philippines. 2 x 2 in.
$10–20

LOT 1003
An invitation
An invitation to a Halloween party, October 31, 2002, given by Morris's close friends, photography agents Rekha Subramanian and Paulo Vitale. 4 x 5½ in.
$5–10

LOT 1004
A group of photographs
Lenore Doolan and her college friend Kyle Kaplan are seen dressed up for Halloween. 6 x 4 in.
$10–20

4

(3)

FIGURE 3.3 Page layout from Leanne Shapton's *Important Artifacts and Personal Property from the Collection of Lenore Doolan and Harold Morris, Including Books, Street Fashion, and Jewelry* (2009).

dressed up for Halloween (Lot 1004). One can assume that Lenore is dressed to attend the party associated with the invitation. The recto side of page confirms this readerly inference: Lot 1005 is a photograph of Morris and Doolan at the Halloween party. The reader's eye sutures the photographic stills in the mode of montage as the accumulation and arrangement of things coheres into a narrative. While a "real" auction book appeals to a buyer, this imitation auction book allows the reader to feel themselves, by creating a narrative, exceeding the consumer role and turning the book back from a kind of advertisement into a literary object that has emotional and cultural, rather than purely financial, value.

Of all the objects on display in this novella, books hold special importance to the couple, the narrative, and the book containing it all. Lenore and Harold were professional writers, and their collection of books attests to their bookish sensibilities and their attachment to each other. With titles by Alice Munro, Henry James, John Updike, Robert Lowell, W. H. Auden, Virginia Woolf, and William James, the books in the catalog identify their owners as literary and play important parts in this object-based narrative. Shapton places at her book's midpoint a page spread depicting only books. The image on the verso side (Lot 1202) depicts "Books on cooking from Doolan's library"; Lot 1203 on the recto side contains "Books on photography from Morris's library."[36] This bookish halfway point is a kind of climax for the novel; the relationship it narrates begins to fall apart thereafter.

We see that the book object serves as midpoint in the bookbound novella and recognize that it also functions as a mediator in the relationship the narrative depicts. Consider the example of Lot 1179, *The Complete Untitled Film Stills*, by Cindy Sherman. The object's description contains details about the artifact—"Fair condition, some wear and earmarking to pages"—followed by information about how this book participated in the human relationship: "Inscribed by Morris to

Doolan: 'She reminds me of you...Merry Xmas 2004, love Hal.'"[37] The book on display serves multiple functions: it is a gift, reading material, and a means of inscribing and communicating feelings. For the diegetic reader of the auction catalog, the book is a potential possession; for the reader of Shapton's novel, the book is a synecdochal message reminding us of the multifaceted value of books in a digital age.

Important Artifacts explores the meaning of its title—how artifacts gain importance. The narrative is built through things, and it shows how things help us connect to people and, as the fictional auction catalog attests, also sever connections to them. Important Artifacts promotes consideration of the specific things on its pages but also about how these things come to matter and acquire value. Two pairs of clogs (Lot 1037), a grapefruit knife (Lot 1057), and a menu (Lot 1135) prove meaningful only in their arrangement and presentation on the page. Shapton's formatting turns individual objects into units (or auction "lots") that collectively suggest a larger coherence. Things gain importance through their connections and contexts, especially when bound into a book. Yet, these situations are subject to change, especially in a digital age.

The feminist theorist Maurizia Boscagli uses the term "stuff" to describe objects "that have enjoyed their moment of consumer allure, but have now shed their commodity glamour—without yet being quite cast aside."[38] Stuff is not trash, because stuff still holds a position of potentiality and promise, ready for newfound aesthetic purposes and affective associations. Important Artifacts is a catalog of stuff but also an example of what can be made from stuff. Diegetically, the book is a souvenir of an auction and of a fictional relationship. It is also an aesthetically innovative bookish object that presents itself as a souvenir of a time before digitization, when human relationships happened through physical objects and handwriting rather than through digital correspondence (texting, social media, email, etc.)—of a time when books served as particularly meaningful things in personal relationships. For the actual reader, the stuffness of bookishness only adds to the pathos that the books within the narrative carry.

The souvenir is a particular type of thing, and it is important to bookishness. "The souvenir speaks to a context of origin through a language of longing," Susan Stewart writes, "for it is not an object arising out of need or use value; it is an object arising out of the necessarily insatiable demands of nostalgia."[39] An object becomes a souvenir when it shifts from being a thing or a commodity to becoming the object for projected desires of a lost past. Like a souvenir that acquires personal meaning only after one returns home from traveling, and only after the immediate memories have dissipated, in a digital age the book acquires new value—becoming a newly "important artifact" when its use value as a reading machine has changed. *Important Artifacts* is a powerful souvenir of the shifting use value of books in a digital age.

Bookishness turns our attention to the materiality of books so that we can appreciate the book as a thing whose thingness and thereness matter—matter in ways we measure through a range of values, emotional and economic. In it-texts that narrate the power of a specific book object, stop-motion animations that depict the book as a living thing, and a beautifully designed bookish book that exploits the artifactuality of the book as an "important artifact," we see how bookishness illuminates the book to be a thing whose materiality matters in newfound ways and for emergent reasons due to the negotiations about presence, worth, and intimacy that shape our contemporary networked world.

4

FAKE

What makes a book real? Nearly every digital interface I use has some kind of bookish reference: a wooden bookshelf on my e-reader, the recorded sound of a paper page turning after swiping the surface of a slick digital tablet. In these ways, digital books and interfaces stage themselves as imitations of a material real, and this imitative quality can make them feel "fake." And they are fake, of course, in that these digital versions are not "there" in the way books traditionally have been. But this experience of fakeness—which, in a sense, is better understood as an uncertainty about where the "real" essence of books lies—is, I will show, central to the contemporary literary. The uncertainty grows more complicated as bookish digital representations return to materiality in ever more elaborate forms: the internet abounds with images of cakes and candles made to look like books, wallpaper and curtains printed with book covers, Christmas trees created by stacking books with green covers into a tall triangle. You can even buy bookish fakery in the form of perfume: "Paperback," a fragrance by Demeter, will make you smell like "a trip to your favorite library or used bookstore. Sweet and lovely with just a touch of the musty smell of aged paper." If you prefer to smell like a new book, you can instead spritz "Paper Passion Perfume," which "captures the unique bouquet of freshly printed books."[1]

Fakery fosters a connection to books in places where they cannot actually be, online and in digital devices, where their thingness and thereness must be creatively rendered. Fakery also operates in the analog world, where physical books do take up space in ways that teach us to see their integration into the digital—to see how the production, distribution, and reception of books is informed by digital processes and practices. In other words, bookish fakery abounds in the twenty-first century in a wide variety of ways and for many reasons—a central one, of course, being that the new representational capacities of our digital era have required a renegotiation of our sense of what counts as real (real presence, real connection) overall. The questions of aura and authenticity that Walter Benjamin raised about "mechanical reproduction" in 1935 are, in the era of digital reproduction, renewed and revisited via bookishness.[2]

This chapter considers the role of bookish fakes, understanding "fake" to designate both the digitized image of a book and the physical artifact of the codex released from its readerly functions. Across a variety of objects spanning a spectrum of aesthetic and affective registers—from high art to full-blown kitsch—I explore how bookish fakery provides a means of establishing a bookish identity and also of fostering community formation around books, when books just might not be real things or actually be there. Such fakery enables books to remain in our digital lives—and thus enables our digital lives to have a recognizable force of realness—even if we are not reading them.

One reason that the contemporary literary abounds with fakes is because the digital operates through fakery—through imitation of a real and originary. This is foundational to the discipline: the father of modern computing, Alan Turing, proposed imitation as the conceptual strategy for computation. In the 1930s he introduced the idea of a "universal machine" that would work through mathematical logic to imitate other media formats.[3] This concept laid the foundation for modern computers to imitate mail service, photography, desktop file systems, telephones, etc. Turing also gave us the means for thinking about artificial intelligence by proposing that a computer could imitate human conversation and thereby fool a human into thinking it was a sentient being. He refashioned a Victorian parlor game into what is now known as the Turing Test, and the rest is a long history from chatter-bots like Eliza (1966) through to science fiction—from *Do Androids Dream of Electric Sheep* (1966) and *Blade Runner* (1982) to *Her* (2013)—probing the question of whether accurate-enough imitation of the human is, in fact, the same as the real.

My daughter sometimes plays her own version of the Turing Test on my phone. She tries to stump Siri, to make the AI fail the test of being a conversational partner. "What's zero divided by zero?" she asks the Apple chatbot. Siri responds with a quippy monologue: "Imagine that you have zero cookies and you split them evenly among zero friends. How many cookies does each person get? See, it doesn't make sense. And Cookie Monster is sad that there are no cookies. And you are sad that you have no friends." Siri fakes being human through humor. She passes the Turing Test by making you laugh and, in the process, forget whether she got the answer right. The sleight of hand (by an AI that has no hands) reminds us that computing is about imposture and fakery as much as computation and veracity. This is not necessarily a bad thing. Siri's entertaining response pleases my daughter—who, of course, always cared more about the form of the exchange than about the mathematical content of her question. Siri's elusiveness shows us what bookishness too demonstrates: that fakery is not separate from the creative, aesthetic, generative, or fun.

Think of the central metaphors early digital interfaces made (and still make) use of: a desktop, a trashcan, that cute, gabby paperclip. All fakes. There are no files or folders in a motherboard and no bookshelves inside a cell phone. These are metaphors, and, as Steven Johnson wrote back in 1997 (a long time ago in digital culture), "metaphors are the core idiom of the contemporary graphic interface."[4] Art, literature, and computer interfaces operate through metaphor, and metaphor "is a cozy word for substitution, for proxy, for not the genuine article."[5] Digital production, unlike mechanical reproduction, promises no original, authentic aura, only executions of code. No real, just fakes. In their foundational book *Remediation: Understanding New Media*, the media scholars Jay David Bolter and Richard Grusin argue that what distinguishes new media is its ability to imitate the aesthetics and interfaces of older media. In other words, new media is about faking or "remediating" other, older formats. Maintaining its identity as "new" by holding in tandem the "old," new media acquires the status of the "real."

The remediation of the book has served a particularly vital role in facilitating the transition to the digital. Indeed, we might say that bookish fakery *enables* the digital. From web*pages* that imitate the format of the printed page to e-readers that incorporate the dimensions of a handheld codex to the visual cue of a page corner primed for turning-as-swiping on a digital tablet and to the iconography of a bookshelf or a file folder to organize data, the visual rhetoric and vocabulary of books serve as an important orientation device for digital culture. Today, when school children (digital natives) learn to read, they might learn about books through digital remediations of them. As Jean Baudrillard predicted decades ago, the simulacra (the fake) supplants the real.[6]

Recognizing the intertwined relationship between books and the digital demands the rethinking of any binary oppositions pitting page against screen and setting apart the bookish from the Web surfer. If the digital operates through bookish metaphors and if bookish folk now rely upon the digital in order to purchase, share, review, and (yes) read books, then we need to take seriously this situation in any effort to understand the contemporary literary. We (especially literary critics and scholars) cannot just talk about stories or books, poetics or formal practices, authors or publishers, without considering the strange, funny, surprising stuff that frames the bookish for us—and that by faking us out, makes us feel connected to books in a digital realm.

Fake books are nothing new. They have been part of the long history of the book since (at least) eighteenth-century decorative spines and outright literary forgeries.[7] Mindell Dubansky, a book conservator for the Metropolitan Museum of Art in New York City, curated a recent exhibition of "blooks" (a portmanteau for "book-look") at the Grolier Book Club in New York City in 2016. Blooks, which have been around since the Middle Ages and had a surge of popularity in the United States during the nineteenth century, are objects that look like books but contain no pages; they are fake books that celebrate "the fake, the flawed clone, parody, imitation, appropriation."[8]

Another type of fake book that has a long history is the "dummy spine." "Many a briefless barrister," said a critic in 1950, "has used dummy books to give an air of established prosperity and learnedness to his chambers, as have doctors to garnish their consulting rooms."[9] In the twentieth century, this long tradition spread out of the professional office and into the private home, particularly after Edward Bernays introduced fake books as décor for middle-class American homes as part of a marketing scheme. Freud's nephew and a pioneer in public-opinion research, Bernays was "commissioned in the 1920s by American publishers to get shelving spaces included in house designs used by speculative builders, so that the

FIGURE 4.1 Example of a "blook," from *Blooks: The Art of Books That Aren't: Book Objects from the Collection of Mindell Dubansky* (2016), 38. Condiment set and miniature book rack.

Source: Permission to use image granted by Dubansky.

rooms would look incomplete unless the eventual owners dashed out to buy books to fill them."[10] And if the primary role of the book is decorative, that role can be performed just as well—one might say, can be "really" performed—by a fake book as an actual one.

Thus for a long time, fake books have been a vital and historical part of the literary and of being bookish. Twenty-first-century culture takes this fact to new lengths. For instance, at Target.com you can purchase a stack of "real" books—with covers, pages, and printed type—presented as a decorative bundle tied together nicely with a twine bow. This stack is sold as an item; its books are not intended to be untied, opened, or read. The spine of each book contains part of a famous quote. In this case, one book's spine states "Paris is always"; the next book, "a good idea"; and the final book "—Audrey Hepburn." When stacked, the bindings collectively spell out the quotation. We read these books by reading their spines and viewing them as a stack—their thingness and their content have melded. A featured "highlight" in the item in its online description states that the bookish décor appears in "neutral hues of white, black and tan," allowing the fake books to blend in anywhere.[11]

"So-called fake things demand support systems," Kati Stevens writes. "Fake flowers get real clay pots and vases; fake fruit real bowls."[12] Yet, fake books are not like fake flowers or fake fruit. As Bernays understood—when he sold fake books in order to sell built-in bookshelves in middle-class homes—books index larger systems of social value and class stratification as well as the infrastructures that support them. Educational curricula, the literary canon, library access, leisure time for reading, etc. are all bound up in the image of a book. Fake books are not just stand-ins for real codexical objects; they also register the systems and institutions that support class distinctions, associations, and ambitions—the conditions that

FIGURE 4.2 A stack of books as home décor from Target.com.

make people want to buy homes with bookshelves so that they can imagine filling them up.

Whenever I give a talk about bookishness and show my array of slides, it is the kitschiest objects that get laughs from the audience. Here, kitschy bookishness means those things that play on the connectedness between the literary and its aspirational commodity forms. The duvet cover decorated with text, especially the image of the lady sitting in bed reading it, is a favorite (figure 4.3). Another item that always gets an appreciative guffaw is the "Pride and Prejudice Vintage Mr. Darcy Proposal by Jane Austen by ForgottenCotton"—leggings printed with text from Jane Austen's novel (figure 4.4).[13] These *Pride and Prejudice* leggings presume that someone will use them for bookish self-construction: to proclaim a bookish sensibility (or *Sense and Sensibility*, if you pardon my wordplay). They suggest that their wearer knows and perhaps has even read Austen's masterpiece—and by association, other canonical classics of Western literature—but they go further to suggest a kind

FIGURE 4.3 Bookish comforter that you can read while resting in bed.

FIGURE 4.4 *Pride and Prejudice* leggings by Brave New Look.

of embodied identification with the novel. Part of the pleasure of wearing the leggings, one might imagine, is the full embrace of the kind of overidentification with favorite books for which women particularly have long been stigmatized.

Yet you don't have to wear or even own these kitschy bookish fakes in order to attach yourself to them—and, through them, to Austen, the community of readers springing up around Austen, and perhaps the canon (or literary culture) itself. All you have to do is post a jpeg of the bookish kitsch to Pinterest, Instagram, or wherever, and that act registers one as bookish, someone who proclaims nearness to books even if no analog book has been read. Fake books operate online as they might in people's homes, and, as the bedspread and leggings demonstrate, they don't have to take a codexical shape. In fact, other forms might signal an even greater bookish intimacy.

When my audience laughs (and they always do) at the *Pride and Prejudice* leggings, that laughter changes the feeling of the room. Laughter creates community around a shared experience and affect. But the laughter can be exclusionary as well as connective, and it can also register ambivalence. There can be pleasure in feeling superior to the people who wear Austen leggings, and there can be pleasure in feeling superior to the people who don't wear the leggings. Fake books are slippery things. They can signal an attempt to foster association with high culture, but they can also signal a disregard for such classist values.

Fakes don't necessarily mean any one thing, and they "don't take anything away from the original, but rather add to it the breadth of its influence on the culture and the individuals with which it comes into contact, second-degree or otherwise."[14] This second-degree nature is particularly important for digital fakes because cultivating bookish communities today happens as much through hyperlinks and mediating algorithms as through the sharing of an actual codex or of ideas in real time and space. The image of those Jane Austen leggings might just contain hyperlinks to Goodreads reviews of the original novel or to *Pride and Prejudice with Zombies* or to college syllabi on Victorian literature. These networks of Austen associations are all available online and able to connect Web users in ways that scaffold literary communities joined (and perhaps supplanted) by algorithms and apps as well as Twitter curators, Instagram influencers, etc.[15]

Recognizing the potential connectedness of the Jane Austen leggings should make us think twice before turning up our noses at them or allowing a loud guffaw to be the final word. Such bookishness kitsch is not the abject of literary culture but instead an important site for it. These objects and images foster a sense of the literary in the age of digitization and support attachments between those of the self-identified bookish ilk. These varied sites and phenomena expand and transform the population previously known as bookish and, indeed, the very category of the literary.

KITSCH

Many of the items just discussed operate to some extent on the level of kitsch. Kitsch is not just about bad taste but also about conflicting values and a changing culture. Norbert Elias identifies the origin of the word "kitsch" as being derived from "sketch," something sold but unfinished, meaning that the term expresses disdain on the part of the maker/seller toward the buyer: "the whole contempt of the specialist for the uneducated taste of capitalist society."[16] Kitsch is dependent upon and intertwined with mass production; it references imitation rather than originality.[17] Elias's definition expresses the disdain for the unfinished artwork and the uninformed (stupid) purchaser of it; other critics, like Hermann

Broch, saw in the nostalgia of kitsch a connection between mass consumption and fascism.[18] Broch's response to kitsch is extreme, but kitsch is always about mediating relationships between classes of people *through* objects. "Kitsch is thus not simply a particular kind of artifact but an artifact imagined and judged in divergent ways of communities in conflict with one another."[19] Yet kitsch can also serve to connect and, specifically for my purposes, shape and form communities. The wearer of those Jane Austen book leggings—or just the sharer of the hyperlink containing them— proclaims her love of books (and it's not a coincidence that so many of these easy-to-ridicule, easy-to fear kitschy objects are associated with women and their bodies) in ways that reach outward to others, both people and websites. Such kitschy fake books generate affective associations and also potentially connect people; they certainly do at my lectures, when everyone laughs at the same, strange, bookish image. These fake, "sketchy" replications of books have real effects for collective experience, just as "real" books do.

Bookish fakery is not just the domain of kitschy stuff but has also been used to great effect by writers of contemporary literature. To make the connections between and across this register of bookish fakes, I turn to J. J. Abrams and Doug Dorst's *S.* (2013), a novel that presents a deliciously fake book as the center of its layered narrative, and then to Aaron Reed and Jacob Garbe's *The Ice-Bound Concordance* (2016), an augmented-reality game with a fake author (an artificial intelligence) that uses a very bookish book as the center of its transmedial network. These are two very different examples of literature—one bookbound and one born-digital—but they each use bookish fakery as a formal conceit and narrative concept. They make us rethink the hierarchical values associated with the "original" and "real" in literary culture. They do so by suggesting a point I have shown emerging elsewhere as well: that the digital age requires such reconsideration because fakery is central to it.

S.

Published in 2013 to look like a hardback novel from 1949, *S.* by J. J. Abrams and Doug Dorst is designed to look like a book that has weathered many human encounters, with ready-made signs of wear and tear, marks of readerly affection and use. The flyleaf carries a red stamp proclaiming "Book for Loan" because the book has supposedly been taken out of circulation from a lending library. All of this is fake. When you begin reading, you see that the book contains a novel titled *Ship of Theseus*, by V. M. Straka and translated by F. X. Caldeira, and its margins are filled with different-colored handwriting. In addition to the bookish fakery printed on its pages, *S.* contains a variety of paper artifacts: newspaper clippings, photographs, postcards, and other souvenirs are sprinkled throughout its pages. These also are all fake (figure 4.5).

Every level of this novel's narrative is about fakes. *S.* depicts two characters—Jen, an undergrad, and Eric, a graduate student in English at Pollard State University (a fake university)—who work together in the margins of the book trying to determine if V. M. Straka, the author of the diegetic novel, is real. In the process, they fall in love. Their intellectual activities, flirtations, and increasing paranoia are depicted in the margins of the book in different colors and writerly styles; Jen writes in tight cursive, Eric in small, capitalized letters (figure 4.6). Within Straka's novel, the text that Jen and Eric annotate, characters also have trouble determining what is real from what is illusion. In this, they are like readers in our real world, who—even knowing that the "book" is a novel—are meant to be lured by its commitment to verisimilitude into a sort of enjoyable readerly confusion.

In the novel-within-a-novel, Straka's *Ship of Theseus*, an amnesiac protagonist named S. sails upon a ship that is continually refashioned and rejuvenated over time, leaving it unclear what

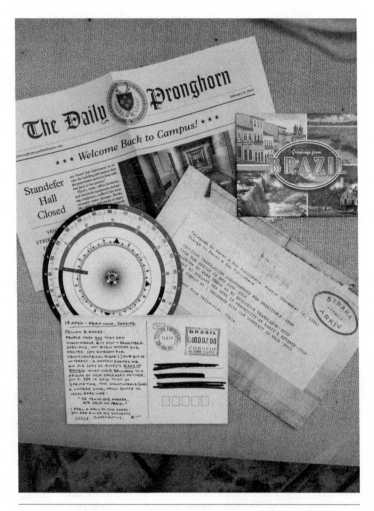

FIGURE 4.5 Slipcover and bookish insert elements from *S.* (2012),
created by J. J. Abrams and written by Doug Dorst.

Source: Reprinted by permission of Mulholland Books, an imprint
of Hachette Book Group, Inc.

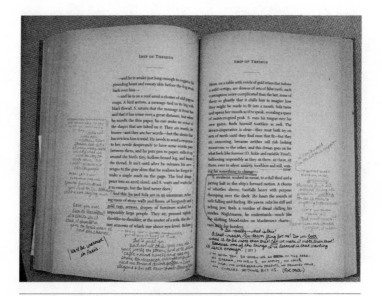

FIGURE 4.6 Fake marginalia in the pages of from *S.* (2012),
created by J. J. Abrams and written by Doug Dorst.

Source: Reprinted by permission of Mulholland Books, an imprint
of Hachette Book Group, Inc.

constitutes the original, or real, ship. "It is entirely possible, S. realizes, and in fact seems quite likely, that not one plank or hatch or
cleat or peg or bolt or nail or rope remains from the night he was
first taken aboard. And yet: this is the ship."[20] The title of Straka's
Ship of Theseus, in whose margins Jen and Eric flirt, alludes to Plu-
tarch's *Life of Theseus* and the ship Theseus used to return from
Crete to Athens, which had to be continually repaired along the
way. "Theseus's Paradox" is a philosophical puzzle that asks at what
point in the ship's history does the original ship become something
different: with which plank of wood or nail replaced to keep the
ship afloat does the real become a simulation of itself? At what

point do we get the fake? The novel *S.* explores these questions in layers upon layers of diegetic play with bookish fakery.

S. allegorizes the question of what constitutes real versus fake within an overtly bookish book that fetishizes elements of "a real book." It contains elements of a real—and even a good—novel and fits within the genre of postmodern metafiction in its use of labyrinthine plotlines, creative page design, and metacommentary. Most reviewers of *S.* focus on these elements of creative fakery, lauding the work for its concept and design. However, they hardly comment on the book's textual content. Perhaps this is because the bookish fakery is what's so good about it. In other respects, and perhaps despite the authors' intentions, *S.* feels like a fake in another way as well: it reads more like an imitation of a novel with complex narrative ideas than a novel with complex ideas of its own. Compared to Mark Z. Danielewski's *House of Leaves*, which offers a considered and ironic critique of overly specialized academic analysis, or Vladimir Nabokov's *Pale Fire*, which renders a full-blown enactment of the intellectual narcissism that can plague obsessive readers, *S* appears as a knockoff, though one done with flair.

S. is also a knockoff in part because of how it was produced. I use the term "produced" intentionally. Authorial credit states that *S.* was "conceived by filmmaker J. J. Abrams and written by" Doug Dorst. [21] J. J. Abrams is the producer and director of such Hollywood television and film blockbusters as *Lost*, *Star Trek*, and *Star Wars*, and *S.* is the product of a Hollywood-style formula for producing content that often privileges visual effect over narrative substance. *S.* does not use its bookish experimentations to reward deep reading and decryption, as does *House of Leaves*. Instead, *S.* falls into the contemporary aesthetic category that Sianne Ngai describes as merely "interesting."

Ngai introduces "the interesting" as "a distinctly modern response to novelty and change." [22] The "interesting," in Ngai's conception, describes art that fails to generate an affective response, works that don't make the reader or viewer care. We might call this the "meh" response, and it proliferates in a culture grappling with information overload. Ngai writes, "The true opposite of 'interesting' is not disinterested but rather an explicitly interested judgment."[23] An interested judgment is one demonstrating strong commitment made after careful review.

Ngai imagines the judgment of "interesting" as a sort of defense strategy for aesthetic subjects in the era of late capitalism. Her book *Our Aesthetic Categories: Zany, Cute, Interesting* considers primarily what this ambivalent judgment tells us about the hypermediatized world of late capitalism, but Ngai's "interesting" also works as a way to describe the limited aesthetic ambitions of "products" like *S.*, whose bookish fakery manifests as symptom of this cultural moment. "The fun of '*S.*' is having the book itself," Abrams states. "To physically hold it is kind of the point."[24] We are meant to have and hold *S.*, not to read and analyze it. It is a work of bookishness that operates as a kind of literary fakeout. Categorizing *S.* as "merely interesting" is not a dismissal but an identification of the work as being of its time. *S.* exploits the capacities of digital printing to simulate manuscript-style elements, and its narrative layers grapple with determining what is real in ways that reflect a contemporary culture awash in fake news.

However, perhaps *S.*'s most poignant mode of fakery is its most innovative quality: the digitally printed handwriting. Handwriting and other acts of marking books have, for centuries, served as means of personalizing and of attaching oneself to the book object.[25] *S.* coyly invites and ultimately refuses its reader the opportunity to personalize the book and make it her own. The pages of this book are already filled with marks from the fictional readers, Jen and Eric, leaving little room for the reader to add anything to the page. We arrive at *S.* belatedly. Readers today are now just as likely to add annotations into a text through digital note-taking software, on an e-reader that mimics the appearance of a book, as they are by hand in an actual book's margins. A sentence from Straka's text is underlined in blue ink, the color of Jen's handwriting, and it denotes a moment of particular bookishness. The underlined text describes a character encountering an old book, " 'A big, dusty old thing.' " The underlined portion reads, "When he opened it, you could smell the musty pages from across the room." Jen's blue cursive marginalia comments, "I've always loved this smell." Eric's small, geometric, capitalized block letters appear directly under her comment: "Me, too. Love how strong it is in the south stacks."[26] The espoused love of the book's smell is contained in a book made to look old, with yellowing pages visually suggesting a potential smell of mustiness. Of course, there is no musty smell to this 2013 publication produced and printed via digital methods. Here the claim to love the smell of books—and to do so within a book freshly printed by digital technologies—is decidedly fake. The fakeness is poignant because it seems to signal an intention to illuminate how any kind of more authentic bookish experiences have been left far behind.

The gambit of *S.* is to lure readers who *want* to remember a time when books smelled, when you borrowed them from lending libraries, and when you actually read them, wrote in them, and spent time interpreting them. Or when you faked it. Of course, for many readers, this time is not past: both old books and careful reading still exist. Nor is it the case that no books today surpass the "interesting" ambitions of this one. What we might say instead is that *S.*, through its intense fakery, works to create the sense that real bookishness was part of the past—even though it can do only so precisely because contemporary digital technologies and production practices enable such beautiful books. Thus *S.* finally, and taken as an imperfect whole, demonstrates how bookishness plays across the boundary of past and present, real and fake, good literature and the merely interesting. What *S.* makes most intensely clear—and helps perpetuate—is the powerful fascination with books that continues into the digital age.

THE ICE-BOUND CONCORDANCE

Computers not only enable bookish fakery; they also read and write. Spam filters, advertising pop-ups, Twitter bots, and automated writing software attest to this fact. Yet the idea of a computer writing the great American novel or understanding a poem has long been a sensitive spot for humanists and computer scientists alike, a source of consternation for cultural pundits. (For a literary example, consider Richard Powers's 1995 novel *Galatea 2.2*, which explores the idea that a computer can pass a master's exam in English literature.) What would it mean for a computer to pass the Turing Test not by imitating a human in a conversational setting but by writing a work of literature that moves us? This is the question posed by Aaron Reed and Jacob Garbe's *The Ice-Bound Concordance*, a born-digital and deeply bookish work of interactive fiction that takes as its starting point the fact that AI can read and write.[27] Through layered narrative and multimodal gameplay, the work promotes consideration about what role is left for humans in the production of literature and bookish culture when computers author books.

The Ice-Bound Concordance is a work of augmented-reality (AR) literature comprising an app downloaded to a digital device and a very bookish book that readers must hold alongside the device in their hands. This transmedia circuit produces two intertwined stories that explore how AI changes the production and reception of literature. The first narrative is an interactive game set in a mysterious research station located in the Arctic. The Carina Polar

FIGURE 4.7 Screenshot from the augmented-reality narrative game
The Ice-Bound Concordance (2016), by Aaron Reed and Jacob Garbe.

Source: Permission granted by artists.

Research Station holds secrets of scientific research and of the lives
lost within it, but it is slowly slipping into the ice. The reader-player
navigates the station's labyrinthine structure and excavates clues
from within it; moving her avatar across the screen's interface
allows her to journey deeper into the station's lowest levels before
the game's time runs out. The work makes full use of ludic techniques for gameplay, turning reading into a game of search-and-
find and taking advantage of multimodal (visual, sonic, gestural,
spatial) aspects of digital storytelling.

The second narrative layer is a metafictional one. The reader-
player must help produce the story of the Carina Station by collab-
orating with an AI named KRIS. KRIS is named after Kristopher
Helmquist—the famous (and fictional) author of a popular science-
fiction novel who, in the diegetic world of *Ice-Bound*, died before

finishing his latest book. That book was destined to be a bestseller, so his publishing company (Tethys House) seeks to cash in on the potential bounty of the novel by acquiring brain scans from Kristopher Helmquist and building an AI based upon them. This AI, KRIS, is tasked with finishing Helmquist's novel. But machine learning requires human input, and KRIS cannot do his/its work alone. Thus, the job of the reader-player is to help KRIS finish Helmquist's novel in order to win the game. You do so by reading Kristopher Helmquist's personal scrapbook, a separate bookish book that KRIS cannot access, and then sharing with the AI relevant content from that book. The personal details contained in the scrapbook provide the necessary data KRIS needs in order to learn the dead author's unconscious plans for the unfinished novel and implement them.

The scrapbook containing the secrets is titled *The Ice-Bound Compendium*, and it is a highly designed art book containing glossy pages that mimic the appearance of a personal scrapbook.[28] As in *S.*, fakery abounds. This is a fake archive of a fictional author but also a fake archive of print culture. The book contains all types of paper-based reading materials: handwritten annotations, Microsoft Word screens scattered with "track changes" annotations printed out to suggest a revision process, screenplay documents, fictional marginalia, 3x5 notecards, magazine cutouts, and more. *The Ice-Bound Compendium* is a decidedly bookish object that uses fake books as a central trope and formal device for highly innovative, interactive digital gameplay.

That this game is about producing a novel—the literary genre most associated with the liberal human subject—is particularly relevant because *Ice-Bound* upends the foundational anthropocentric assumptions of literary culture.[29] Its narrative suggests that machines can write and read books; humans are not the only ones capable of such high-level, humanistic efforts. Formally, you read and play this sophisticated game/novella by using an elaborately

FIGURE 4.8 Bookishness in the pages of Aaron Reed and Jacob Garbe's *The Ice-Bound Compendium*, the book component of the transmedial, augmented-reality narrative game *The Ice-Bound Concordance* (2016).

Source: Permission granted by artists.

designed book, but instead of reading its content, you scan its pages with a digital reading device. The book's pages contain QR codes that trigger the projection of narrative content. The digital technology scans first, processing and translating the book's data (contained in the QR codes) and then projects text for the human to read. This work of literature about an AI tasked with writing a novel thus positions the computer as its primary reader.

Among the many ghosts haunting this work, the most threatening is not that of the dead author Helmquist, of his stillborn novel, or of the scientists who lost their lives in the sinking Carina Station. Rather, it is the ghost of the author-figure—the central presiding premise upon which Western literary production has been based for centuries. *Ice-Bound* challenges the idea of the human as the sole author and source of literature as well as the human as the sole reader of it. Computers—those "imitation machines"—can now read and write, and the literary is transformed by this fact.

Today, authors use computers, word-processing software, and even AI mechanics to produce literature.[30] *Ice-Bound* explores the implications of this fact, pushing us to consider what it means for machines to do more than just finish our sentences or suggest alternative words. The premise that a publishing house can simulate an author's cognition and writing style through digital data collection is hardly speculative in an age of biotech, big data, and personalized AI agents like Alexa and Siri. So what are the implications of the fact that, as *Ice-Bound* demonstrates, twenty-first-century readers not only read *through* computers, using the machine as medium, but also *with* them as co-cognizers?[31] *Ice-Bound*'s narrative about completing a novel using digital technologies and a zombified author is not science fiction but the very real state of the contemporary literary condition.

Ice-Bound's posthuman ghost story, especially when paired with S.'s fabulous fakery but merely interesting narrative, promotes recognition of how the digital inspires creative bookish literature and commentary on its future. Considering *S.* and *Ice-Bound* together through the paradigm of bookishness links them to the vast array of other bookishness objects that circulate in digital culture. Moving from these literary works back to the types of bookishness fakes that opened this chapter—from dummy spines to blooks to those Jane Austen leggings—we can see how our digitally networked culture fosters a critical perspective of attachment to books and literature *through* fakery. Recognizing the importance of bookish fakes, knockoffs, and the merely interesting opens new pathways for criticism—for analyzing the flotsam and jetsam of literary culture and, moreover, recognizing these things to be deeply connected to and mutually constituted by literature. Fake books and bookish kitsch foster bookish identity and community in ways that fortify our bookish future by helping us transition to the digital without leaving book culture behind.

5

WEAPON

Bookishness extends beyond kitsch objects, Web content, and mainstream literature to cutting-edge and avant-garde narrative. Experimental literature employs bookishness in ways that make literature new and raise questions about the impact of new media on contemporary society. In what follows, I read two formally innovative novels that were both starting points, albeit in different ways, for my study of bookishness: Mark Z. Danielewski's *House of Leaves* (2000) and Steven Hall's *The Raw Shark Texts* (2007). Each of these novels exploits their codexical format in ways that draw attention to the materiality of the book and many of the issues explored in previous chapters. What is new here is how these novels allegorize fears of the invisible and viral ways that digital information moves by presenting, through formal innovation on the page, the book as *the* means for illuminating and responding to these threats. In the hands of these gifted authors, the book becomes a weapon against digitization.

The Raw Shark Texts and *House of Leaves* contain surreal narratives about monstrous, mutating beasts—allegories of the computer as a programmable and changeable "imitation machine" (as Alan Turing called it).[1] Both novels contain different types of horror stories, but they each operate in the tenor of a mind-bending thriller. They reflect a deeply felt sense that the digital is changing our lives in unforeseen and unfathomable ways, and they position the book medium—that discrete, stable, and self-contained object—as a kind of weapon against disembodied data and "flickering signifiers."[2] These are not easy beach reads but difficult narratives that require a high level of attention and interaction. Both novels invite readers to spend hours decrypting narrative puzzles and wondering what is real. They promote close, hermeneutic reading, the kind associated with literary criticism, as they engage in extraordinary typographic play, page design, and labyrinthine, hypertextual narrative. These exemplary works of bookishness literature make us appreciate the power of the book in the age of the digital.

HOUSE OF LEAVES

I begin with Mark Z. Danielewski's *House of Leaves* (2000) because this book is an essential foundation for bookishness. *House of Leaves* was published in 2000, and much has been written about the avant-garde novel since then, and for good reason; it is now part of the twenty-first-century literary canon.[3] *House of Leaves* employs a variety of formally experimental narrative techniques—typographical play, a complex hypertextual structure organized through an elaborate system of footnotes, and brilliantly innovative page design. The book is also, as we will see, a hub in a transmedial network that incorporates the internet in ways that extend its hypertextual narrative to other media forms. In what follows I present *House of Leaves* as an early example of a bookishness novel that allegorizes fears of the digital and the power of paper-filled books to safeguard against changing times. Needless to say, the lessons *House of Leaves* teaches about books and bookishness read differently in 2020 than they did in 2000. Reading *House of Leaves* today invites a means of tracing how the aesthetic of bookishness has developed and became mainstream.

The novel is composed of an extensive narration of a film by a blind man, Zampanò, who dictates his critical commentary about the (fictional) documentary film "The Navidson Record" by the Pulitzer Prize–winning photographer Will Navidson.[4] The film chronicles Navidson and his family's horrifying travails living in a house whose insides grow larger than its frame. The house's hallway mutates into a cavernous labyrinth that devours sound, light, direction, and human beings. In this novel, one of the twenty-first century's first gothic novels, the house emerges as a horrifying monster, upending ideas of the home as a safe space. The titular and horrifying house at the heart of the novel is not only the one owned by the Navidson family in the narrative but also the book that houses the pages (or leaves) that describe it.

Zampanò's pseudoscholarly examination of "The Navidson Record" film is edited and annotated by Johnny Truant, who discovers Zampanò's manuscript after the blind man's enigmatic death. Truant is a psychologically scarred but highly literary misfit who encounters Zampanò's manuscript as a collection of multimedia scraps: "Endless snarls of words . . . on old napkins, the tattered edges of an envelope . . . legible, illegible; impenetrable, lucid; torn, stained, scotch-taped."[5] Truant pieces these discrete fragments together and weaves in his own narrative layer through a set of footnotes that describe his hyperactive sex life, traumatic childhood, and devastating experience editing Zampanò's text.

Truant's version of The Navidson Record is then edited by the corporate (also fictional) entity the Editors, whose presence is noted by the monosyllabic "-Ed." Proceeding in an objective tone that contrasts with Truant's highly emotive commentary, the Eds. produce an additional set of footnotes that demarcate emendations to the text and acknowledge missing information. Each of these narrative voices is identified by a different font and associated with a specific medium: Zampanò's academic commentary appears in Times Roman, the font associated with newspapers and the linotype; Truant's footnotes are in Courier, which visually reference a typewriter's inscription and thematically identify him as the middleman, the "courier" of the manuscript; the terse notations from the Eds. are aptly presented in Bookman. The novel unleashes this arsenal of typographic elements in ways that turn the reader's attention to the book's materiality and the powerful possibilities of its codexical elements. The typographic taxonomy is just one part of the novel's elaborate experimentations in bookish play and page design.

For instance, a page describing the house on Ash Tree Lane is presented as a physical wall containing a window. A square appears on the recto side of the page, inserted into vertical columns of text (figure 5.1). The square is outlined in blue, and this blue box contains a long footnote listing architectural items not present in Navidson's house: "Not only are there no hot-air registers, return air vents, or radiators."[6] Turning over the page shows the backside of the window, now on the verso side; its text appears backward in the square frame, as if the page itself has become a physical wall around which the reader maneuvers. Through this incisive act of design, the novel blurs the boundaries between Navidson's house on Ash Tree Lane and the house of paper leaves (the physical book) that contains it. The reader sees the book from a new angle, literally, because the reader has to turn the book around and flip its pages back and forth in order to see how the section operates. What makes this book so mindblowingly innovative is how it takes the thing we think we know—the book—and exploits its physical capacities in ways that make us see and appreciate it anew.

In the early years of the new millennium, I wrote about *House of Leaves* as a networked novel, a cutting-edge work that engaged its bookish format in ways that connected it to the internet and

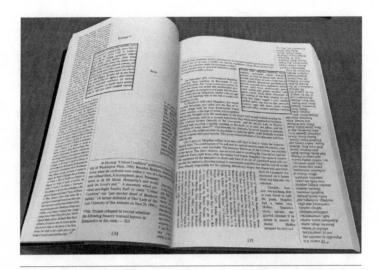

FIGURE 5.1 Excerpt from *House of Leaves*, the remastered, full-color edition, by Mark Z. Danielewski (2000).

invited readers to navigate between the book and "the *House of Leaves* website (www.houseofleaves.com), *The Whalestoe Letters* (an accompanying book by Danielewski containing a section from the novel's Appendix), and the musical album *Haunted* by the author's sister, the recording artist Poe."[7] Back in 2006, I wrote, "Mark Z. Danielewski's *House of Leaves* (2000) is a novel that is not just a book."[8] My article argued that the 709-page codex embraces and exploits the pleasures of print in typographical play and innovative page design to explore how practices of reading are changing in a digital, transmedial age.

When the novel was first published in 2000, these transmedia efforts were quite innovative. *House of Leaves* linked up to the internet through the URLs on its covers. Beneath the copyright and publisher's information is a web address for the official *House of Leaves* website: www.houseofleaves.com. Sharing the title of the novel and its publication date, the website was the book's fraternal twin. On the book's back cover is a red circular icon surrounded by text that prompts the reader to "listen to the house . . . 'HAUNTED' the new CD from Poe on Atlantic Records. www.p-o-e.com." The text identifies "the house" from the novel as distributed across media forms and prompts the reader to pursue these connections between book, website, and album.[9] Back in 2006, I wrote, "I read *House of Leaves* across its multimedia network to show how the novel uses its assemblaged narrative to teach the reader to engage with a contemporary print novel that is distributed across the digital network."[10] I understood *House of Leaves* as not only experimenting with transmedia storytelling but also as serving a pedagogical purpose, particularly for bookish readers: to connect books to digital networks in ways that demonstrate the power of books to withstand medial change.

Much has changed in the last fifteen years. *House of Leaves* still works across a transmedial network, but this fact is no longer novel, so to speak. The concept and operations of transmediality no longer require the kind of careful explanation I gave it back in 2006. That essay explained and modeled how to take seriously comments on an online bulletin board and also how to consider the relationship between these paratextual media forms and the main, bookbound narrative. Today, transmedia narrative is now a central aspect of contemporary culture; we binge-watch *Game of Thrones*, based on George R. R. Martin's novels, by streaming it through a television hooked up to the internet, while at the same time seeking out more information about the episodes on Twitter and blogs. Reading across media platforms is part of daily practice. Yet my understanding of *House of Leaves* stands: the novel aestheticizes its bookish format in ways that prompt readers to recalibrate the role and value of the book within a digital, transmedial network. My opening claim from that 2006 article—"*House of Leaves* (2000) is a novel that is not just a book"—now needs to be updated to make clear that its book-ness, and indeed its bookishness, is precisely what continues to make *House of Leaves* so important.

Written during the internet boom of the 1990s and published during the dot.com crash, *House of Leaves* reflects its digital environment. The novel's hypertextual narrative imitates the internet in its bookbound pages, and every appearance of the word "house" is colored blue, the color of an active hyperlink on the internet.[11] These colored signifiers are textual acts of "remediation," the term Jay David Bolter and Richard Grusin use to describe how older media, such as books, "refashion themselves to answer the challenges of new media."[12] Formally, the novel is structured as a hypertext, a system of interconnected narratives woven together through hundreds of footnotes. The novel aestheticizes the power of the codex to contain numerous stories, voices, fragments, and media forms. The book acts as an "imitation machine" (like Turing's computer) that mimics other media, especially film and the web; its appendix contains representations of filmstrips, napkins, photographs, and more. Remember that in 2000, fears about the death of the book proliferated, and Y2K was a seen as a very real threat because of concern over data loss.[13] *House of Leaves* exploits these fears from its opening pages.

The novel begins with Johnny Truant warning the reader, "Old shelters—television, magazines, movies—won't protect you anymore. You might try scribbling in a journal, on a napkin, maybe even in the margins of this book. That's when you'll discover you no longer trust the very walls you always took for granted."[14] The old shelters are old media, which are no longer adequate cultural protectors and guardians in the face of digital technologies. In the horror story found in *House of Leaves*, it is the mutation of these "old shelters" that proves most terrifying. The man-eating house whose insides exceed its walls is certainly one scary monster, but so too is whatever bloodthirsty shadow haunts Johnny Truant. As Truant promises in the first pages of this massive novel, the real threat is what exceeds the novel's narrative and bleeds into real life: fear that our old shelters—the book-based systems we "always took for granted" in enabling shared knowledge, systems of authority, and cultural values—have been breached.

The real ghost in the film, and the novel that subsumes it, is the "spectre of digital manipulation." The first line of Zampanò's manuscript states, "While enthusiasts and detractors will continue to empty entire dictionaries attempting to describe or deride it, 'authenticity' still remains the word most likely to stir a debate." The reason the authenticity of this film looms large, so large that it is introduced in the first paragraph of the book within a book, is because of the threat posed by digital technologies. The text continues, "This leading obsession—to validate or invalidate the reels and tapes—invariably brings up a collateral and more general concern: whether or not, with the advent of digital technology, image has forsaken its once unimpeachable hold on truth."[15] The digital destroys the ability to believe in photography as a realistic representation of the world. "The referent has become unstuck," William J. Mitchell wrote in the days of early digital photography.[16] The idea that digital manipulation of imagery can generate fake news and unhinge the concept of authenticity, let alone the cultural structures (for example, newspapers and professional journalists) for validating authentic imagery, was not yet commonplace in 2000. There was no Facebook or Twitter, and cell phones with surveillance technologies were not yet in everyone's handbag. It was a different time. Danielewski's novel signaled a cultural shift, and it did so through a focus on books.

A key moment in the narrative occurs when the characters recognize that something is irrevocably wrong in the house, when they see the symptom of the monster; this happens through an encounter with a book. Upon returning from vacation, the Navidson family finds that their house has inexplicably grown, and a new closet has emerged inside it. Will Navidson does the rational thing and takes measurements. He concludes that the "width of the house inside would appear to exceed the width of the house as measured from the outside by ¼." Will asks his brother Tom to prop open the closet door. Tom does so with a book. "Tom turns to Karen's shelves and reaches for the largest volume he can find. *A novel.* Just as with Karen, its removal causes an immediate domino effect." The wall has expanded beyond the length of the shelf, and the books fall to the floor. "This is exactly when Karen screams."[17] The chapter ends. It is the extraction of a novel from a bookshelf that causes the books to fall and expose the horrifying transformation that has occurred inside the house. In this metacritical moment, *House of Leaves* identifies the bookbound novel as a means for measuring and registering a changing reality.

At the time, I viewed *House of Leaves* as demonstrating how the book and bookbound literature is strengthened, not threatened, by the emergent digital network. This remains true, but something has changed. Today what is remarkable about *House of Leaves* is not its transmedial but its bookish aesthetic. I would amend the first line of my original essay on the novel to now read: "Mark Z. Danielewski's *House of Leaves* is a novel that is very much about its status as a book."

THE RAW SHARK TEXTS

The Raw Shark Texts was another important starting point for my study of bookishness because my first published article on the topic was about this novel. The article was based on a talk I gave for the University of Michigan's symposium "Bookishness in the Digital

Age" in 2009. (Yes, dear Reader, I stole the title.) The brilliant and generous Jonathan Freedman organized the event and asked his speakers to address the following questions: "What new literacies are generated in the digital era? What happens to older cultural practices and norms associated with and generated by the traditional book? And most importantly, how are institutions—libraries, presses, and universities—to negotiate this new situation?"[18]

I was eight months pregnant and a brand-new professor. I was talking about the importance of the book's body at a moment when I was acutely aware of my own. I addressed the audience not only with a very large belly but also full of optimism that literature like *The Raw Shark Texts* made books matter more than ever before. I performed a close reading of Hall's novel and shared the stage with scholars I idolized.

Leah Price talked about book history and Alan Liu about media theory. Fears about the digital permeated that conference. It was 2009, and the world was grappling with this new thing called a Kindle. During Q&A, a local bookshop owner and audience member wanted to know what we—as professors of literature and presumed lovers of books—were going to do to stop the threat to local bookstores. I had no concrete answers and could only return to the literature for suggestions. I argued that *The Raw Shark Texts* shows how the threat of digital demise just might be a good thing because it propels innovative literature and aesthetic rejuvenation. I claimed that this case study was not singular but exemplified a larger strategy that I called an "aesthetic of bookishness." Ten years later, I still think this is true. Though, as this book demonstrates, I now see the aesthetic of bookishness as far exceeding the realm of experimental narrative.

The Raw Shark Texts employs bookishness to critique a central ideology of digitality: that a message can be divorced from its medium, that content can be separated from its form, data from its

body. N. Katherine Hayles has shown how, historically, when cybernetics and information studies laid the foundation for digital technologies and computational culture, "information lost its body"; "it
came to be conceptualized as an entity separate from the material
forms in which it is thought to be embedded."[19] The belief in disembodied digital information enables AI and supports, as Alan Liu
argues, a "religion, as it were, of text encoding and databases."[20] *The
Raw Shark Texts* demonstrates the dangers of ideologies based in
the belief of transcendental data by exploiting the format, materiality, and aesthetics of the codex.

The novel begins with a lesson about the importance of embodiment and materiality. "I was unconscious. I'd stopped breathing."
When the novel's protagonist Eric Sanderson recovers his breath,
he notices an envelope addressed to him and containing a typed
letter: "First things first, stay calm." It is signed, "The First Eric
Sanderson." The novel thus begins with a character reading and
breathing himself back to life, making these two embodied actions
synonymous and intertwined. The fact that the letter is typed on
paper rather than printed out or viewed on a digital screen sets the
tone for the novel's privileging of the material and embodied over
the digital and disembodied. The narrative's focus on physical, analog things continues when, once revived, Eric takes stock of his surroundings: "I noticed little lived-in things." "The limescale on the
kettle, the half-used bottle of washing-up liquid. The couple of
pieces of dried pasta in the gap between the fridge and the kitchen
units. All the marks of use." These things are, the text continues,
"Signs of life."[21] *The Raw Shark Texts* begins by focusing the gaze of
both its protagonist and its reader on the thingly and artifactual.

The central threat in this novel is the personification of disembodied, digital data in the form of a terrifying predator, the
Ludovician shark. The shark attacks Eric in the novel's beginning,
leaving him unconscious and without memory. This is not a

normal, flesh-eating shark—the iconic kind that strikes horror into the hearts of generations raised watching *Jaws* (to which the novel presents an explicit homage near its end). The Ludovician is a conceptual shark, a metonym for digital data that swims unseen across invisible depths, platforms, and interfaces. In the process, the shark destroys all possibility of privacy and sense of safety. The shark is a perfect predator for the posthuman information age. It is attracted to "pure thought, pure concept," ideas not grounded in artifacts, where "there's no physical anchor.'" "Numbers and math" attract the shark; it feeds off of information that is unmoored from physical instantiation. When the shark attacked Eric, "The idea of the floor, carpet, the concept, feel, shape of the words in my head all broke apart on impact with a splash of sensations and textures and pattern memories and letters and phonetic sounds spraying out from my splashdown." Eric nearly drowns in the whirlpool of logos until he grasps something of substance: "A vague physical memory of the actuality of the floor."[22] Physicality saves him.

Eric fends off the shark with things, the most powerful of which are books. When the Second Eric Sanderson awakens from an attack, he finds himself in the strangest—or the likeliest, if read through a paradigm of bookishness—of places: "I found myself inside the lower part of the living room bookcase, the upper part having broken apart and collapsed, leaving me avalanched in books."[23] The bookshelf serves as a shelter and a stopgap. The books on the shelf surround Eric and save him from further attack. The scene references contemporary bookish and bookwork sculpture, including the Columbian artist Miler Lagos's *Home*, an installation in which a human-size igloo-like shelter is made completely from books.[24] A few pages later, the novel makes the point even more directly. The First Eric Sanderson advises the Second Eric Sanderson in how to fortify himself against the shark using, yes, books as bricks: "Build the books into a small wall around yourself. My notes say three to five books high is best."[25] *The Raw Shark Texts* teaches us to surround ourselves with books.

The novel not only tells the reader but also *shows* her that books are powerful weapons against disembodied data. When the shark at the center of *The Raw Shark Texts* finally appears, when it makes itself visible to Eric and to the reader, it does so as concrete poetry (figure 5.2). For the characters in the novel, this is a terrifying transmogrification of the invisible into the concrete. For the reader of the novel, the transformation of fictional shark into semiotic word sculpture turns attention to the book as a powerful material medium. Words are suddenly not just concepts but are also black ink arranged on a paper interface. The page is seen to matter, and the novel about a shark circling at unknown depths becomes possible only because the codex containing it has layered pages bound together to give it depth.

It soon gets even better. The pages between 328 and 373 depict a brilliant moment of bookish reflexivity, wherein the diegetic depths take on physical manifestation as the Ludovician shark emerges. The verso page is left blank, while the recto page depicts the slow, page-by-page emergence of the shark, from a tiny spot (early in the pagination sequence) to a full-blown visualization of an open-mouthed predator (on page 373; figure 5.3). Readers hold the book and flip the pages in the style of old-school animation. The novel imitates early cinema in ways that demand that the book be looked at, not just in and through. This scene also posits an appreciation of the book as an archival medium because this book is shown holding the history of film and also a killer, concrete-poetry shark.[26] The novel depicts the book as an archive that is also as a weapon against digital memory loss caused not only by corrupt files and technological obsolescence but also by information overload, which overwhelms our ability to historicize and remember.

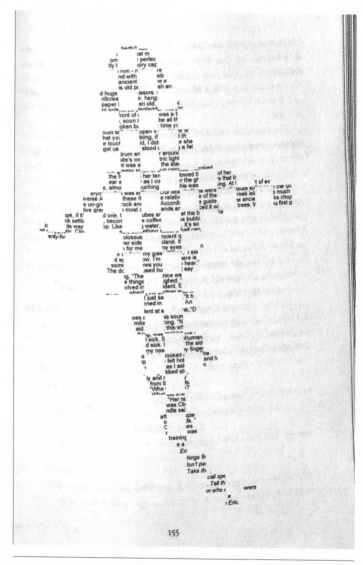

155

FIGURE 5.2 Concrete-poetry shark in Steven Hall's *The Raw Shark Texts*
(2007), 155, whose appearance illuminates the page as interface
in the book medium.

FIGURE 5.3 Flip-book sequence of a shark emerging from depths, across pages 328–73, in Steven Hall's *The Raw Shark Texts* (2007).

Source: Reprinted by permission of Canongate Books. All rights reserved.

The shark at the center of *The Raw Shark Texts* feeds off of characters' minds, devouring their memories and leaving victims as mindless physical shells. A letter from the First Eric Sanderson laments, "I used to know so many things . . . all I have are splinters. Remains of things I was quick enough to write down and preserve." What was written down remains; paper preserves and books safeguard. Eric shuns the use of computers out of fear, following a clue from his former self: "There is no safe procedure for electronic information. Avoid it at all costs."[27] In contrast, the book—the nondigital reading machine—allows for safe handling of its data because this content is embodied in a discrete (non-networked) medium.

When Eric decides to fight back against the monsters of the digital, he prepares by reading a book. From the pages of *An Encyclopedia of Unusual Fish*, Eric discovers that in Native American myth, the shark was understood not as devastating predator but as a valuable archive: "Each Ludovician shark came to be revered as a self-contained, living afterlife" because it contained the "memory-families" made from "generations of shared knowledge and experience." Something has changed. Today, "the streams, currents and rivers of human knowledge, experience and communication which have grown throughout our short history are now a vast, rich and bountiful environment."[28] More information is streaming faster and more fluidly across communication networks that are more connected than ever before. McLuhan's "global village" is now a fertile feeding ground for the Ludovician shark and other monsters like it.[29] Like an identity thief or internet predator, the shark uses the vastness and complexity of the Web to seek and stalk its prey.

Like a shark that terrifies because its actual physical location is unknown until its fin breaks the surface of the water (cue John Williams's two-toned music), the Ludovician represents and preys upon the fears about how digital data operates. Our lack of knowledge about how digital technologies and protocols actually work produces a fear of the unknown. Whereas computers of the 1980s and 1990s possessed a DIY aesthetic—clunky brown boxes with their screws facing outward, inviting tinkering—Apple's innovation was to offer sleekly designed products that hid the nuts and bolts. The iMac series (1998) exemplified this change (even though its back was translucent) with computers that were sleek art objects framed in smooth white plastic—not to be messed with.[30] Hiding, or, to use the language of the novel, *submerging*, the operations of computers renders them harder to know. As technological upgrade culture hastens, our external memory archives—hard drives, storage software, and the ubiquitous cloud—become less tangible and *there*.[31] In this scenario, physical books become symbols of safety and nostalgia; their thereness anchors us to a sense of the knowable, and there is serenity in that feeling.

The shark is not the only predator in the novel, nor is it the only representation of digital systems and the threats they pose. The larger evil is the yin to the shark's yang: the completely disembodied entity named Mycroft Ward. Ward was once a living person, a gentleman scientist who lived at the end of the nineteenth century and devised a computational method to stave off death so that he could live into the twenty-first century.[32] Ward produces a kind of Turing Test: "Through the use of thousands of questions and tests, Ward succeeded in reproducing a very rough copy of his personality on paper."[33] He successfully standardizes this informational pattern into an algorithmic program that can be endlessly replicated. The postindustrial logic and operating method succeeds,[34] and Ward extracts his identity from his material substrate—his body—so that he can circulate as a form of disembodied data, entering the bodies of others like a kind of computer virus and parasite. With the outbreak of World War I and its industrialized warfare, Ward realizes the threat of possible destruction to his host body and decides "one body was simply not enough to guarantee his survival," so he "modified the original personality recording template" to enable "one Mycroft Ward, a single *self* inhabiting two bodies."[35] His cognitive program spreads virally and globally, leaping across bodies and decades, spreading out into an invisible global network. Ward becomes the ultimate posthuman, cybernetic monster.

Mycroft Ward (hear, of course, "Microsoft Word" but also Mycroft Holmes, Sherlock Holmes's older brother) invites critique of megacorporations that seek global dominance through the invisible traffic of information over digital networks.[36] To name the novel's villainous virus after Microsoft's word-processing program reflects concerns about the displacement of writing from ink on paper to digital data and software. The name also suggests that writing is not just creative but also technological.[37] To substantiate these interpretations, Ward's backstory is presented in a distinct format on the page, setting it apart and drawing attention to its materiality. Eric hears the tale of Mycroft Ward from his companion, Scout, who tells the story orally, but Ward's story is presented in the novel not in the form of dialogue but, rather, as a separate document titled "The Story of Mycroft Ward." This formal detail and documentary aesthetic focuses the reader's attention on *how* a message is presented, and it plays upon the idea—posited throughout the novel—that the printed record is trustworthy, particularly in contrast to the digital. The formal presentation of the Mycroft tale suggests that the book is a valuable medium for archiving and thus defending against the kind of memory loss produced by digital, mind-eating villains such as Ward.

Following the advice of his former self, Eric seeks the assistance of one Dr. Trey Fidorous; his quest leads Eric to an underground labyrinth and very bookish shelter called "un-space."[38] Access to the un-space is a gateway located in a bookstore. The house of books that serves as a portal into the safe space of un-space is described as "sort of religious." It is here, in this book-based shelter off the map of the digital grid, that Fidorous hides in a refuge built completely from books: "The walls themselves had been built from more solid material than we'd seen previously—hardback books mainly, with the odd thick softback dictionaries, thesauruses, textbooks—and had been constructed with careful bricklaying techniques." This space too, like the bookstore, is described as a sanctuary: "It's like a church or something."[39] This bookbound place becomes the center of resistance and rebellion wherein Fidorous, Eric, and Scout (Eric's accomplice and romantic interest) stage their last stand against the evils of disembodied, digital information.

To combat digital monsters, Eric and his crew use books as weapons. One of the many letters Eric Sanderson receives from his former self informs him that books of fiction are the best type of weapon against the shark. That is because fiction does not offer a direct download of data (like numbers and math) but instead distorts the information channel, through which the Ludovician travels, with literary poetics (like metaphor) and formal innovations of the type we see on the pages of Hall's novel. The novel depicts bookbound literature as the greatest weapon against the digital because it confuses data-seeking predators by presenting information in complex, poetic ways and by building layers of literary and figurative meaning that act as a "labyrinth of glass and mirrors."[40]

As the novel's title implies, this narrative is about making meaning through print-based acts of analysis. When said aloud, *The Raw Shark Texts* sounds like "Rorschach test," the famous psychological examination that prompts an individual to interpret the appearance of an inkblot on paper; the test's administrator then assesses the given answer as a means of interpreting the individual's psyche. The reference to the Rorschach test is a reflexive reminder that the reader of *The Raw Shark Texts* is making meaning from ink blots presented on the page, not just from transcendental ideas and concepts. Data must be embodied to be meaningful. *The Raw Shark Texts* teaches this lesson and exemplifies how bookishness responds to digital threats through innovations in literature.

Whether Mycroft Ward, the Ludovician Shark, or the house on Ash Tree Lane, the monsters of the digital lurk as invisible, specter-like, and seemingly disembodied. As in any good horror story, it's the thing you know is there but can't see that is the most frightening. In Hall's novel, the digital threat comes from unseen depths, whereas in Danielewski's the monster is just behind the halfway-opened hallway door. These allegorical narratives illuminate the fact that we don't know—and worse, might not care—how digital media work. These novels challenge the idea that the digital will displace books, and they do so in formally experimental texts whose bodies demonstrate the durability and renewed potentiality of the book medium. They also caution us to think about the media we use, including the book. *House of Leaves* and *The Raw Shark Texts* exploit the possibilities of the printed page and the codexical medium in novels that allow readers to face their fears *in* literature and *through* books.

6

MEMORIAL

Bookishness is a form of memorial. It registers a sense of loss, promotes remembrance, and supports the formation of identity and communities around these feelings. Jonathan Safran Foer's *Tree of Codes* is one of the more innovative and rich examples of bookishness memorial.[1] This work of experimental literature and innovative book design alters the Polish-Jewish author Bruno Schulz's *The Street of Crocodiles* (1934), a poetic and surreal collection of short stories about a family in a small European town experiencing changes caused by increased urbanization and modernization.[2] Foer reworks Schulz's expression of a world in the midst of tremendous change, updating it for the contemporary moment. He does so by using a digitally enhanced process of die cutting to carve into Schulz's book, extracting from its pages words and phrases and leaving behind holes on the page. The result: a strange, beautifully bookish thing.

Rectangular gaps of various sizes puncture the pages of *Tree of Codes*, producing a latticework of paper upon which words or strings of words form islands around the holes (figure 6.1). As Foer constructs them, the holes on the pages become memorials that hold space for the reader to consider and reflect upon what is missing. Schulz was murdered by the Nazis, and his writing was largely

FIGURE 6.1 Image of page layout from Jonathan Safran Foer's die-cut book *Tree of Codes* (2012), design by Sarah de Bondt, published by Visual Editions.

Source: Permission to use image granted by Visual Editions.

lost to history. The sense of loss—the loss of people, books, and cultural memory—permeates *Tree of Codes* figuratively and formally.

Foer's writing-as-cutting process is not only a memorial to Schulz's text but also to Foer's own reading of it.[3] The relationship between *Tree of Codes* and *The Street of Crocodiles* is not one of translation but of remixing and remembering. What is remembered here is multiple: Schulz's texts, the People of the Book lost in the Shoah, and the artifactuality of the codex in a culture of digitization. In describing the impetus for his poetic, bookish die-cut experiment, Foer writes, "On the brink of the end of paper, I was attracted to the idea of a book that can't forget it has a body."[4] He approaches the book as a medium of remembering (one that "can't forget") and of a particular type of remembering (that "it has a body") for a particular age (digitization, "on the brink of the end of paper"). Foer produces a memorial to the book in a book that exemplifies bookishness.

Books have always served a memorial function. Their codexical structure is a storage medium for text as well as other objects: flowers, letters, fabric swaths, etc. The book has also long been imagined as a prosthetic device that extends human memory, an archive of human expression and history. As we have seen in previous chapters, digital technologies and practices change how books are made and used as well as what books signify and mean. In turn, these changes inspire bookishness memorials like *Tree of Codes*, which testify to a sense of loss and provide a site of remembrance for a medium that itself has historically acted as a memorial.

READING THE BOOK

We are meant to look at, not just in or through, *Tree of Codes*. Published by Visual Editions, whose tagline is "Great Looking Stories," the cover design is artistic, intentional, and worthy of closer scrutiny (figure 6.2). The white background displays rows of round black dots, more like smudges or inky fingerprints than perfect circles, and they are arranged in a line. When viewed from afar they take on the effect of a pointillist painting or a highly pixilated image. The blots suggest handicraft or even hands (and digits), bodies behind the smudgy traces, but they also signify digital data. We can read the dots as referencing punch holes of early computing machines (think of a music box, player piano, or Jacquard loom). This punch-hole programming method later shifted to binary digits in digital operations, and Foer's cover suggests a recognition of this medial transition. The author's name and title are interspersed across the dots, with the letters standing apart from them, as if the

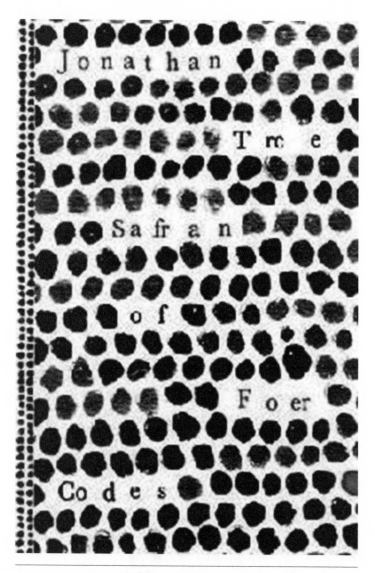

FIGURE 6.2 Front cover of Jonathan Safran Foer's *Tree of Codes* (2012), designed by Jon Gray for Visual Editions.

Source: Permission to use image granted by Visual Editions.

text has been decrypted from censorship. The cover design of *Tree of Codes* primes the reader to read for what is missing as well as what is there.

When you open the book's cover, you face a wall of empty bricks—but not blankness. The first page of *Tree of Codes* contains no text, just holes. Vertical columns of gaps are piled atop one another. The stack of excisions marks the absence of previously readable paragraphs. Above the gaps are two smaller boxes: a little rectangular hole below which a single square is cut out, both center justified. We know what goes here: a chapter or story title. This gap is an indexical sign, a silent monument testifying to the presence of lost elements. This detail also calls attention to the relation between, in Jerome McGann's words, "the linguistic code" (literature's content) and "the bibliographic code" (literature's physical structure), which combine to produce "the textual condition" of printed surfaces.[5] Foer thus begins his book by illuminating the media-specific protocols that arrange information on the page and shape readerly practices.

You read this book, as you read all books, by isolating a page from those behind it. But this is where the similarities end. The die-cut process leaves the pages fragile, so you must carefully extricate each page without ripping it. Words from pages behind the one at hand appear through the gaping holes, so you must carefully hold the individual page in order to isolate it and read the text it contains. Only then does the page serve its traditional use value as a tool for reading.[6] Since words on the page only appear—or, more precisely, the words from other pages only disappear—when you turn the page, you notice the physical action involved in turning pages; you see how, once turned, the very familiar act of interacting with a book takes on new meaning. The media theorist Espen Aarseth used the turning of pages as his cornerstone example of what constitutes "trivial" interaction, in contradistinction to the true interactivity of video games.[7] Yet in *Tree of Codes*, the act of turning pages becomes a highly interactive and meaningful activity.

Indeed, the turning of pages transforms this book's appearance. The verso side of the page is always blank. This design decision becomes poignant as the reader moves through the book. The page's blank backside is a physical location for building spatial objects through the accumulation of paper; rectangular shapes emerge as pages build up on the verso side, allowing for the construction of mutating and sculptural cavities that increase in depth and shape as more pages are turned and added. As layers of paper accumulate, the diegetic spaces described in the text, printed only on the recto side of the page—the mysterious rooms in Schulz's stories—attain visual figuration in the shadow-filled cavities on the blank verso side. Foer uses the architecture of the codex to create meaning that is visual, physical, and spatial.

The irony here is that this bookish object is decisively dependent upon digital technologies. To carve his codex, Foer employed a digitally enhanced process of die cutting that required intricate technical production and an elaborate partnership between the London-based publishing house Visual Editions and expert printers in Bruges.[8] A short video released by Visual Editions, "Making *Tree of Codes*: 3 Months in 3 Minutes," depicts the use of industrial machines programmed to produce the fragile pages and artisanal aesthetic of Foer's product.[9] As a result of this process, a mass-produced paperback looks like an artist's book; the digital enables the bookish.[10]

Foer describes his creative process: "At times I felt that I was making a gravestone rubbing of *The Street of Crocodiles*, and at times that I was transcribing a dream that *The Street of Crocodiles* might have had."[11] Yet when we watch the movie about making the book, we do not see the author writing or painstakingly carving out single words. The video shows no hands gingerly rubbing, no fingers

feverishly writing. What we see instead are large machines programmed to perform an encoded digital sequence, operating
mechanically and quickly. We see a post-digital scene of publishing.
Because the reality of the production process involved advanced
technologies, Foer's insistent claims that his creative method was
intimate and analog can be read as a decisive claim to bookishness.

Florian Cramer uses the term "post-digital" to describe a cultural moment wherein "'digital' has become a meaningless attri-
bute because almost all media are electronic and based on digital
information processing."[12] We live in a post-digital world, one in
which digital is now the norm. The result is cultural ennui toward
the digital and nostalgia for older methods, not just pre-digital
methods but also earlier digital ones. Post-digital generates desire
for the early days of the digital, when glitch aesthetics and the like
still stunned and amazed. *Tree of Codes* is a post-digital object produced by digital practices to create an aesthetic of bookishness, one
that memorializes and fetishizes a cultural moment before digital
ubiquity— when we were "on the brink of the end of paper" and
when bookishness was born.

READING THE TEXT

To understand the text of *Tree of Codes*, the reader must circum-
navigate the holes and tease out meaning from the fragmented
narrative they compose. We open with a fairytale-like, somnambu-
list moment when "whole generations/ had/ fallen asleep" and
"The passersby—/ had their eyes half-closed." The book's formal
technique creates a parallel universe; we prick our fingers on the
sharp edges of the cut paper and wake to the materiality of the
book. We see the paper's color, feel its texture, and register its fra-
gility. "Only a few people noticed—/ the—lack of color, —/ —as in

black-and-white photographs—" in the sky. The unobservant others are too "exhausted by—/ —passivity—" and "—,—/ —the poses
and postures—/—,—/— the—/ —shifting—weight from foot to
foot" to see the color behind the colorless sky or to recognize their
own stasis. *Tree of Codes* makes present the material but nonmedial
aspects that we usually cease attending to when using the book as
a medium for reading. The narrator observes that the sky was an
"anonymous gray" because it has a "—, a screen—placed to hide
the true/ meaning of things—,—/ a façade behind which there was
an—/ overintense coloring—."[13] Like the narrator, the reader sees
anew the elements that form the material world, specifically that
of bookbound literature.

Tree of Codes begins with an apocalyptic moment: "An enormous—/ last—day—of—life."[14] The specific date and place is not
given, nor are characters' names, and this refusal to locate enables
the poetic and fragmented narrative to unfold with a sense of allegory and operate as a universal memorial. This is the last day of life,
but it is also an infinite day. The narrator and his mother walk
through the streets of their town, where "children—greeted each
other with—masks—painted/on their faces." These imitations of
life and normalcy reflect a deeper lack, a "growing in this emptiness" represented by actual gaps on the page. "Apart from them—
mother and I ambled." Set apart, these two "passed—houses" that
are "sinking, window and all, into—/ their—gardens." Their walk
occurs on "an endless day, An enormous—/ last—day—of—life." The
threat of death permeates: "Hours pass—in—/ coughs." Time is
measured by the physical symptoms of sickness until "that ghost of
a /smile—/ fell away—and—receded—/ and—finally faded." This
first loss is probably the mother's death, although "those—distant,
unseeing eyes"[15] are not identified, and the fragmented nature of
the text makes it extremely difficult to summarize a coherent plot.
But neither coherence nor narrative is the point here.

Reading this text is not just about making sense of linguistic signifiers. To the extent that *Tree of Codes* tells a story, it is one of generational shift. The old world is on the verge of slipping away while
a younger generation comes into its own. We see this in the tale of
the narrator awakening into his own identity as a writer. In stun-
ning prose made all the more so when one considers the constraints
that produced it, Foer describes the evolution of a writer: "Something stirred in—me," our narrator explains, "i/ loosened one of the
planks/ —, opening a window to—/ a new, wider world." The windows open out into the world and allow our narrator to see it anew.
The narrator's response: "I—/ —wrote—/ in a notebook, —added it
all up—." He becomes aware of himself in a new way: "the only living and—knowing thing—/— was—/— me—." He is "—shaken—into
consciousness—, my/— sense of smell and—hearing sharpened/
extraordinarily." The reader experiences a parallel awakening, real-
izing an ability to make sense of the holey pages as her senses have
been "sharpened extraordinarily." The narrator states, "—i—/—
would rise from the table—and peer/ through the keyhole—."[16]
There is an analogy here to the reader's experience of peering
through the holes in the pages of this book. The reader is placed in
the position of the narrator/writer/new generation and is provided with an allegorical lesson in how to read with a focus on
media, material formats, and infrastructures: the keyholes and not
just what is seen through them.

Reading *Tree of Codes* is also a practice of toggling between presence and absence. Indeed, *Tree of Codes* illuminates and aestheticizes the binary of presence and absence, the concept that scaffolds
digital code. We can consider the holes on the page using N. Katherine Hayles's seminal interpretation of binary code; she suggests
that the zeroes and ones enabling informatics can be reconsidered
through a paradigm of pattern/randomness instead of presence/
absence.[17] Seen this way, the holes are not just absence or lack but

patterns that produce pregnant pauses, inform reading pace, and invite reflection. Read this way, the holes in Foer's pages reference digital information and a relationship, not opposition, to printed literature.

We can read the die-cut gaps in *Tree of Codes* as indexically referencing the history of print, specifically the evolution of the page as interface. Blank spaces only emerged on the page during early manuscript culture, far before the invention of the printing press. "In the West, the ability to read silently and rapidly is a result of the historical evolution of word separation that, beginning in the seventh century, changed the format of the written page, which had to be read orally and slowly in order to be comprehended."[18] The separation of words facilitated faster and silent reading practices. Previously, script ran across the page; this *scripta continua* required readers to vocalize the text in order to understand (orally) the words being read (visually). *Tree of Codes* harnesses the power of blank space on the page, but instead of encouraging a reading practice of silence and speed, this book promotes slowness, vocalization, and repeated reading. Here, the blank spaces—both the holes on the page and the white spaces left on the paper between words—result not in readerly ease but in challenge and confusion. The gaps are too extreme. They disrupt the normal reading practices of print and instead memorialize pre-print textuality.

When read aloud, in the style of *scripta continua*, a narrative emerges. Consider an example from a page just before the death of the narrator's mother. The word "her" occurs five times (out of twenty-five words) on this page and on four different lines; its presence is significant. Yet it is only when the page's text is read aloud that the word's reoccurrence becomes rhythmic, inescapable, and even hypnotic. In an oral performance of the page, "her" takes on an aspirated quality, sounding like breath and demanding the exhalation of it.[19] "Her" emerges as central to the narrative action rather

than merely as a descriptor. The embodied performance illuminates the importance of the mother in the text, supporting Hayles's
computationally derived but similar conclusion: "'mother' appears
four times more frequently than in the original, making up 0.42% of
the words."[20] At the bottom of the page, the single word "her" sits
alone, centered in an otherwise carved-out block. The word is the
sole occupier of space and meaning. The presentation of "her"
turns the signifier for the ailing mother into a physical signified
and a memorial to her loss. The importance of vocalization is made
all the more poignant by the repetition of language about silence
appearing on the preceding pages: "the silence talked"; "the bright
silence"; "the/ secret of—private time"; and "the silent/ —sighs."
The words describe silence but demand sound. At the very moment
when the narrator sees his mother's body as a surface, interface, or
medium to read ("her—eyes reflected—the garden"),[21] the reader is
reminded of the physicality involved in reading the page, a page
presented as a memorial to her.[22]

The text ends with loss but also with apocalypse averted. We
learn that "the world was to/ end." Rather than depict people in a
state of panic and lamentation, however, this apocalyptic promise
bestows significance on the lives of those living in anticipation of
change: "Something— had entered our lives/—. An importance
permeated our—/ sighs—." Like the moviegoers at the end of
Thomas Pynchon's Gravity's Rainbow (1973), Foer's citizens await the
end, in this case an approaching "fatal comet." They prepare for a
"simply incredible chance—/—, an honorable end." The end comes
when the comet that had been approaching Earth and threatening
destruction simply passes by, and "life returned to its normal
course."[23]

If we take the comet as a metonym for the doomsday scenario
described in polemics about the impending death of the book in
Y2K and all that it signifies (the end of reading, knowledge, an

informed democratic citizenry, etc.), then Foer's narrative ends by showing that such fears are overblown. Before the comet spurts its last fiery and fearful promise, the text asks, "What was there to save us?" The next line offers a response. The all-powerful father figure, the archetypal giver of life and poetic inspiration, is resurrected: "my father— was the only one who/ knew a secret escape— /— his eyes closed." The escape is a refusal to fear destruction: "Father saw/ no/ comet, leaving the comet behind." When "Left to itself, it —withered away amid —/ indifference." The threat of destruction withers from inattention. What remains? The text's last line returns to the father as a means of concluding: "my father alone was awake, wandering silently/ through the rooms." A gaping hole follows this last sentence.[24] This rectangular space, a physical room on the page, provides a place for the reader to wander after the text has run its course. It is a material figure and presence, a place and a memorial. *Tree of Codes* ends by showing how paper pages and holes punched into them produce meaning even after the last word of the text is long gone. The architecture of the book and the infrastructure of the page remain and remember.

READING THE BOOKWORK

Tree of Codes challenges genre categorizations; it is literature, sculpture, monument, adaptation, translation, and more. This hybridity (and confusion) of identity might explain why it is left out of the "Also by Jonathan Safran Foer" list in the prefatory page of his most recent novel, *Here I Am* (2016). Most critics and readers simply don't know what to make of *Tree of Codes*.[25] They see it as a failed experiment in book art or conceptual poetics. They complain that its cut-from-another-source idea is a gimmick. Michel Faber's review for the *Guardian* is exemplary: "Snip seven letters from the title *Street of*

Crocodiles and you get *Tree of Codes*—and so on, for 134 intricately scissored pages"; later, "All very interesting, but I suspect that this book will be appraised more as an artefact than as a story."[26] A rip-off of Oulipian procedural poetics or Williams Burroughs's cut-up method, perhaps, but there is something else going on in Foer's book. *Tree of Codes* strives not for allegiance to a conceptual poetics (think Georges Perec's *La disparition* [*A Void*; 1969] and its missing *e*'s) but instead toward illuminating the artifactuality of the book in ways that promote appreciation and memorialization.[27]

Approaching *Tree of Codes* as bookish memorial enables us to read this book as (and alongside) altered book sculpture and book-ish Holocaust memorials. Exemplary here is Micha Ullman's *Library* (1995), located in Berlin's Bebelplatz, the infamous spot where the Nazis lit their book-burning pyres. This subterranean memorial presents an illusion to the viewer standing above it at street level: when you look down into the small square of glass, you see what appears to be endless empty bookshelves reaching to unknown depths. This poignant memorial suggests a parallel between the bodies of books and the bodies of people, both of which burned in the flames of the Shoah. As we know from Heinrich Heine, whose famous words mark the simple plaque in Bebelplatz denoting the spot of the otherwise missable monument, a society that burns books will also burn people.[28] The parallel between the bodies of books and the bodies of people also permeates *Tree of Codes*, rhetorically and in deeply material ways. Indeed, *Tree of Codes*, with its radical alteration of Schulz's text and its memorial aesthetic, can be read as a Holocaust memorial and as Holocaust literature.

Tree of Codes can also be read as bookwork. *Tree of Codes* is not alone in its formal practice of cutting up an older book to make a new art object that turns our attention to the materiality of codexical media. There is a long history of such practice and scholarship on it, as Ed Ruscha's and Dieter Roth's oeuvres and Johanna

Drucker's scholarly *The Century of Artists' Books* illustrate.[29] *Tree of Codes* is often considered in relation to Tom Phillips's *A Humument* (1973), which alters the pages of the Victorian novel *A Human Document* (1892), by W. H. Mallock, to produce a new work of bookbound visual art. But there is an important distinction between *Tree of Codes* and *A Humument*. Whereas Phillips treats the pages of a Victorian book, adding sketches to them in order to produce a visual palimpsest, Foer extracts from the physical page to expose the material skeleton that comprises literature's body. Foer's *Tree of Codes* more closely resembles the carved bookwork of the book sculptor (or "book surgeon") Brian Dettmer than the overpainted pages of Phillips's artist's book.[30]

The last two decades have seen the proliferation of bookwork sculpture that uses books as the material substance for three-dimensional art.[31] Artists such as Doug Beube, Cara Barer, Su Blackwell, Long-Bin Chen, Brian Dettmer, and Kylie Stillman create artistic memorials to books by altering them—carving into them or folding their pages, twisting, shaving, or otherwise altering their bound form.[32] The literary scholar Garrett Stewart identifies bookwork as part of the genealogy of conceptual and readymade art: "the book itself as 'study' rather than as functional object." For Stewart, it is no coincidence that bookwork emerges now, in a digital moment: "The book in a museum is what all books may become."[33] *Tree of Codes* might not qualify as bookwork, since it is not handcrafted and singular, but it does "simultaneously celebrate and forewarn the viewers of the fine line between monuments and ruins."[34] I read *Tree of Codes* as a kind of mass-produced bookwork, at once memorial and ruin, sculpture and literature.

By briefly considering a few of Doug Beube's bookworks as exemplary of the genre, we can see connections between bookwork and Foer's bookishness that illuminate the complex historical interplay of codex and memorial. Beube, a pioneer in conceptual bookish art since the 1980s, has experimented with the book's status as sacred object and memorial site across a wide variety of projects. *Feast* (1993–ongoing) is an installation piece that displays a nightstand with its drawer opened. Inside the drawer, a bible, submerged in honey, is opened to a page of Ecclesiastes with the famous passage about seasons of change. The ongoing work drips honey onto the bible, enacting the slow transformation of the book from sacred object into crystallized organic matter.[35] In contrast, *Interfaith* (2002) is a sculpture made from a bible whose pages have been sliced along the horizontal axis to enable a braiding, overlapping of paper. The Oulipo-like effect (à la Raymond Queneau's *Cent mille milliards de poèmes* [1961]) enables a mix and match of content and an interactive reading experience.[36] Seen together, the two works create sculptural memorials to and from sacred books in the Western tradition and play with the sacredness of the object.

Or consider another of Beube's bookish memorials, one built from less sacred content. *Twin Towers* (2007) is a 9/11 memorial in which two columns of books are stacked on steel tripods signifying the two World Trade Center towers destroyed by hijacked airplanes. The books are carved so that their cores stack as a circular column; the book objects appear as architectural infrastructure, scaffolding for metaphoric buildings. The 9/11 memorial displays books as building blocks and archival structures, physical remainders that remind us to remember.

One of my favorite of Beube's works is from his Twister series, in which he twists books in ways that transform them into fantastical objects. *Inside Macintosh* (2005) uses a Macintosh user's manual as its source material, turning it inside out in a way that "slyly alludes to this cultural and technological passage from print age to electronic age as it transforms an inevitably obsolete Macintosh user's manual into an art object."[37]

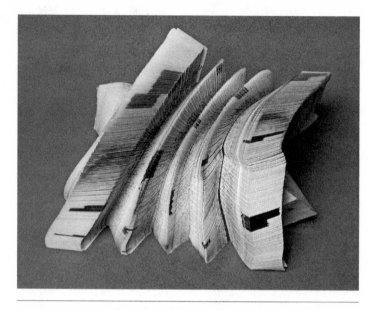

FIGURE 6.3 Doug Beube's altered-book sculpture *Inside Macintosh* (2005).

Source: Permission to use image granted by the artist.

These bookworks by Beube explore the book as matter for memorializing, whether it's Judeo-Christian theology, the tragedy of 9/11, or Mac user practices circa 2005. "My art creates a moment of meditation," Beube states; it "is not about binding but about context and how the book sits in space."[38] Beube thus distinguishes his work from artist books, which are about their bound content. The meaning of the encounter with bookwork is based not in content but in context, the space and time in which the viewer sees the book and contemplates its presence. Beube aligns bookwork more with memorials than with literature. *Tree of Codes* picks up this aspect of bookwork, making us rethink how we read it so that we can consider its bookish body as a thing in space and an object about time.

READING THE AFTERWORD

In his afterword to *Tree of Codes*, Foer develops a complicated context for his bookwork. In this concluding text, Foer identifies Schulz's *The Street of Crocodiles* as his favorite book, expressing such reverence for Schulz's prose that he claims to have suffered a kind of paralysis in the face of attempting to engage with it: "So many of Schulz's sentences feel elemental, unbreakdownable. And his writing is so unbelievably good, so much better than anything that could conceivably be done with it, that my first instinct was always to leave it alone."[39] Foer does not leave it alone. He chips away at *The Street of Crocodiles* to create *Tree of Codes*. If we recall that the word "codex" comes from the Latin word for "wood" (which described the wooden planks used as covers to straighten and safeguard the parchment or vellum pages of ancient books), we see Foer carving his *Tree* from Schulz's codex in both a material and figural sense. Inspiration is here depicted not just as transcendent (as in a Romantic sensibility that figured the Muse as fleeting), as psychological (as in an internalized Harold Bloom–ian anxiety of influence), or as textual (as in the Derridean sense of writing as the trace of an always-already absent presence) but as material, embodied, and bookbound.[40]

When we look at the material actualities of this bookbound homage, however, we see that Foer lied—or at least he cheated a little. *Tree of Codes* is *not* actually carved out of Schulz's book. Foer's authorial claim—which centers (and sells) the work and upon which most readings of it are based—is deceptive. "Working on this book was extraordinarily difficult," he writes, because "unlike novel writing, which is the quintessence of freedom, here I had my hands tightly bound. . . . Every choice I made was dependent on a choice Schulz had made."[41] Foer's statement elides certain material truths. First, he neglects to tell us that his book, "whose meaning was exhumed from another book," was actually mediated by a third book: the English-language edition by Celina Wieniewska published by Penguin in 1963.[42] "Foer remembers Schulz," Rebecca L. Walkowitz points out, "but, like most anglophone writers, he forgets about Polish, and thus he allows his readers to forget about Polish, too."[43] A focus on *Tree of Codes* through the angle of bookishness allows us to see Foer's project as serving less to memorialize Schulz or Polish literature than the medium in which he and Schulz both publish. Reading *Tree of Codes* as a memorial to books exposes how Foer's artistic process is less about language and words than it is about the medium of the book.

A bookish focus enables us to see the ramifications of Foer's second deception: he did not carve his text directly from his source material. Foer fails to tell us that before die cutting Schulz's book, he and his design-publishing team translated it (in a material sense). They turned Schulz's pages from double-sided displays into single-sided textual interfaces. As I have already explained, the text in *Tree of Codes* does not continue across the front and back (recto and verso) of the page but instead appears only on the recto side. This simple detail has great significance: it registers an act of medial adaptation that dramatically alters the page and its poetic performance. This transformation enables the paper-formed layers to appear, deepen into cavities, and mutate into geometrical shapes on the backside of the page. Recognizing the medial translation necessary to produce this aesthetic effect illuminates Foer working against the grain (to continue the woodish puns) of Schulz's codex. He uses *The Street of Crocodiles* and the die-cut technique to draw attention to the book as medium and artifact, but he doesn't actually use Schulz's book to do so.

Foer's sleight of hand continues. The title for his afterword to *Tree of Codes* is "This Book and The Book." "The Book" in Foer's title references the holy book (actually five books) associated with "the people of the book": the Torah. "The Book" also, of course, references Schulz's *The Street of Crocodiles*. Foer suggests one more possibility for the meaning of "The Book": The Western Wall in Jerusalem. The Wall is a remnant of the destroyed ancient Second Temple; it is a ruin, a memorial, and a sacred place for pilgrimage. Visitors to the Wall traditionally place handwritten prayers into the cracks between its massive boulders. Because of this practice, Foer describes the Western Wall as "a kind of magical, unbound book."[44] Through this associative logic, Foer positions the wall he has built—a wall composed of die-cut blocks on the page—in relation to the Western Wall. Foer inserts *Tree of Codes* into a sacred triad of books, alongside Schulz's and the Western Wall. In so doing, he elevates his own creation and illuminates the intertwined relationship between memorial and fetish object.

Memorial, as Emily Apter reminds us, is a kind of fetish. "Fetishism fixes in time and place—commemorating a founding moment in the etiology of consciousness, harking back as a 'memorial' (Freud's expression) to an unrepeatable first form."[45] If we remember that the etymological origins of "fetish" come from "making," then we can see Foer remaking *The Street of Crocodiles*—a work that is itself about the making of the modern subject under industrialization—into a bookish fetish object that commemorates a founding moment in the omnipresence of digitality: when we thought we were "on the brink of the end of paper."[46] *Tree of Codes* is a memorial to the past (to Schulz, the Holocaust, manuscript reading practices, and more) and also to books in the age of e-readers.[47]

The bookish memorial that is *Tree of Codes* not only fetishizes the book as object and turns its die-cut holes into synecdochic fetishes, but it also adapts a work by a famous fetishist. Bruno Schulz had a fetish for women's feet, particularly those encased in high-heeled shoes.[48] More importantly for our purposes, Schulz's writing and visual art is full of book fetishism. One need only to read the powerful short story "The Book," wherein the young narrator is compelled and obsessed by one of his father's books, identified as only "The Book."[49] Schulz's biographer, Jerzy Ficowski, sees "The Book" as a trope and symbol for understanding Schulz's larger oeuvre: "The creative reconstruction of that 'Book' is Schulz's major literary postulate."[50] The title of Schulz's book of drawings, *The Booke of Idolatry*, signifies his book fetishism. "When Schulz writes of books, which are both sources of myth and myths in themselves, he calls them *księgi*" because "a *księga* is a great sacred ancient book, like the books of the Bible."[51] When Foer selects Schulz as his source for his bookish memorial, he is doing more than just picking a favorite text: he is creating the ultimate bookishness fetish object and memorial.

Tree of Codes is a memorial to books in and for the twenty-first century. Its physical presence and formal aesthetics operate like a bookwork, promoting reflection on the book's contemporary context. Its poetic textual content requires deep attention and care. It is a work that generates consideration of the roles and purposes that books serve and how those roles might change. It also registers the much longer history of the book, a history full of transformations in page design and reading practices. The result is a beautifully bookish thing, a fetish object and memorial that can be admired as literature, sculpture, design, and cultural commentary. *Tree of Codes* demonstrates how bookishness turns the book into an art of the present that archives and memorializes the past.

CODA

My daughter just became a reader, a real reader. Or, rather, this was the thought I had—that her reading had become "real"—when she first finished a novel that she truly loved and didn't want to end. After devouring the book, hardly lifting her eyes from the pages, she slowly closed its covers. Aware that her time within its pages was now over, she looked up at me. Her eyes were wide and full of sadness.

I felt sadness too, for her but also for me. I used to read like that too. I'd sit for hours, content in silence and isolation, profoundly attached to a story, enjoying the irresistible pull of a book in my hands. When I watch Sydney read, I feel nostalgia for a time before I adopted the skepticism of adulthood and the critical lenses of academic training, before cell phones with colorful screens stole my attention away from books, and before I felt like I never have enough time to read for pleasure. This pleasure, as Sydney was experiencing, always contained loss within it, and that awareness of loss made the pleasure more palpable and powerful. There was nothing about the critical apparatus I brought to the moment—the recognition that a long cultural and media history made me privilege *this* particular image of immersive, childlike emotive reading as "real," instead of many possible others—that made me value it less. My desire to think through the question of what made some reading feel "real" propelled my study of bookishness.

When it comes down to it, bookishness is about the complex bundle of emotions that come with recognizing that a relationship to books has changed—this relationship, for many readers and writers, is both personal and cultural. As we saw in the previous chapters, artists grapple with their feelings about this recognition across a range of genres, aesthetics, and media—from bookwork sculpture to bookish films, bookbound literature to kitsch. Bookishness expresses apocalyptic concern and technophilic glee. It binds otherwise disparate nodes into a network and a cultural constellation that shines so brightly it cannot be ignored.

For literary critics like myself, taking bookishness seriously means changing how—and perhaps what—we read. I value Sydney's novelistic immersion while also recognizing that her encounter is not the only "real" textual encounter and not even the only one that might usefully be counted as "literary," however we might register that elusive term. The literary today relies on the internet, the infrastructure that shuttles users between websites offering books to social media groups discussing them. We can no longer just analyze text and image but must also address text that functions *as* code, metatags, and hyperlinks—the language that generates attachments between Jane Austen's novels and those kitschy leggings. We must also adopt a networked paradigm that attends to the real and changing material conditions, contexts, and experiences of emergent literary culture. What this means for how we design courses, produce scholarship, or judge our own prose is not yet determined but imperative to consider.

Bookishness reminds us that the literary is not only about stories, formal aesthetics, and the love of books but always also about human connection. While researching this book, I found connections to others, online and in person. Social media connected me to folks with specialized interests in the history of paper and fake books, people who generously shared their knowledge in tweets and emails, bolstering my research. Facebook algorithms also found bookish kitsch for me, reminding me how the research process and experience changes as it moves online.

I also connected with people offline and in real life, for I wrote this book as a series of talks, given at conferences and universities around the world (I've been very lucky!). It was at such events that I befriended the bookwork artists Doug Beube and Brian Dettmer, who taught me to see books differently—to love them for their sizes, shapes, colors, and chemical compositions and also to see them in relation to visual art. Smart audiences asked rigorous questions that helped me refine my instinctive understanding of my object of study. Such events remind me of the power of the in-person—the way that different things are possible around a table than they are via video chat—even as they often revealed how mutually imbricated "real" and "digital" connections are. (This lesson seems particularly powerful and pertinent after the Coronavirus global pandemic of 2020, with the sheltering-in-place orders and virtual living it mandated.)

Online connection often brought me to in-person experiences, and the in-person would generate more connection online afterward. Often, after a talk was over, audience members would send me links to relevant articles and pictures of their own bookish things (a forearm tattoo of a bookstack and wedding cake shaped to look like a bookshelf were my favorites). This back and forth between real and virtual expanded my archive and awareness of bookishness as well as my sense of attachment to a community constructed around it.

My study also connected me to my own daughter, the newly minted reader. *The Land of Stories: The Wishing Spell* (2012), by Chris Colfer, was the novel she was reading. *The Land of Stories* is a popular series of books for young readers that adapts well-known characters from fairy tales, weaving their stories together by locating them all in the same fairytale land and updating their messages with feminist sensibilities. As my daughter pointed out, *The Wishing Well*, the first in the series, is very bookish. It centers on a magical, animated book—the definition of a fetish object. Alex and Connor, young twins, are mourning the loss of their father when they are given a book titled *The Land of Stories*. This book proves to be a magical portal through which they escape the real world and fall into a diegetic story world filled with fairytale characters. If my daughter is any indication, young readers have a parallel experience.

When Alex, the more bookish of the twins, opens her copy of *The Land of Stories*, "the room lit up from its golden glow." To test the book's magic powers, she drops a pencil into it "and watched it disappear." Sure enough, in an *Alice in Wonderland*-like moment, "Alex lost her balance and fell—headfirst into the book!"[1] This pivotal scene exemplifies central aspects of bookishness explored in previous chapters: bookbound literature is shown to be a place of refuge from grief (chapter 2); the book object is animated and anthropomorphized into a thingly fetish object (chapter 3); remediation and fakery—here, of clichéd and remixed storylines—proves surprisingly catchy and also necessary (chapter 4); the book is a weapon for staving off real-world threats (chapter 5); and the work memorializes by archiving older literature in a narrative about books within a book (chapter 6).[2]

Watching my child read that book was sad but also deeply satisfying and profound in ways that exceeded the moment itself. Studying bookishness has helped explain why. The literary scholar and book historian Patricia Crain explains that the image of the child reader became a powerful cultural symbol in the late nineteenth century, when new conceptions of childhood merged with and propelled newly forged bourgeois aspirations.[3] The industrial revolution of the nineteenth century and the digital revolution of the twentieth/twenty-first each produced their own types of fetishization of this image. The image of the child reader suggests a cultural need for children to read but also "that they should be *seen* reading."[4] Adults like me, estranged from our own experiences of immersion, need to see the child, the embodiment of the future, reading a book in order to know that reading—and books too—have a future. The image is an expression of hope and promise; it is also an act of archiving that memorializes a bookish past and its reading practices in ways that sustain them.

I opened this book with my Mac BookBook, the laptop cover made to look like a leather-bound book. I said that this codexical computer case spurred my study of bookishness, but the ideas were percolating (as they often do) years before. In 2007 I was strolling down the main drag of Silver Lake, Los Angeles, window-shopping with a friend. We entered a tiny store filled with all sorts of cute, palm-sized objects printed with clever sayings and eye-catching type. One stood out. A small writing pad, about two by four, pale yellow and white, with the header "Paper E-mail" (figure C.1). The notepad contained the usual components of an email (to, date, time, cc:, bcc:, subject), along with boxes to check beside the following words: send, attach, reply, forward, spam, and trash. Below these options, a large white rectangle welcomed a handwritten message. At the bottom of the small page, an open signature line. A paper email—how smart and funny and strange! The object felt like a gravity well of media history; it pulled my attention to the potential of printed paper to register the impact of the digital. This memo pad, imprinted by and imagined for the digital, was so much more than a pad of sticky notes. I held it for a while, fascinated. I felt an immediate attachment to this thing that offered back the fantasy, in thing form, that we never relinquish our connections to the

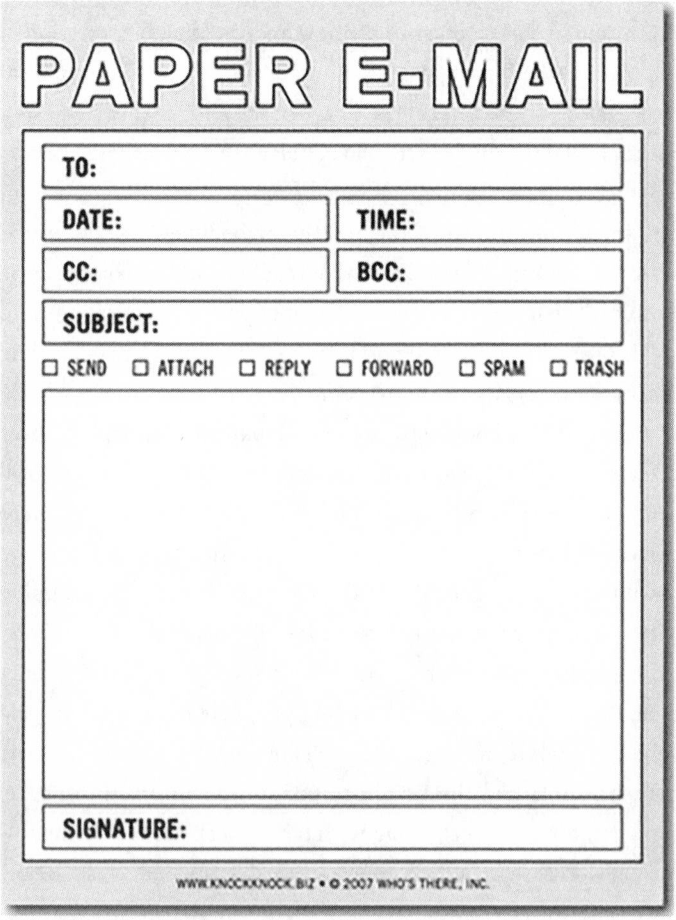

PAPER E-MAIL

TO:	
DATE:	TIME:
CC:	BCC:
SUBJECT:	

☐ SEND ☐ ATTACH ☐ REPLY ☐ FORWARD ☐ SPAM ☐ TRASH

SIGNATURE:

WWW.KNOCKXXNOCK.BIZ • © 2007 WHO'S THERE, INC.

FIGURE C.1 Paper email, a stack of Post-it notes designed to imitate the email form.

past—to older media and ways of connecting, communicating, and remembering. I purchased it and put it on my bookshelf. It has remained there for over a decade.

I have never once used a single page from the notepad. It has sat intact, facing me from the bookshelves in my offices at two different universities, on two different coasts of the United States, challenging me to decipher its meaning and explain the pull it had over me. The notepad has become a focal point for my study of bookishness. Printed in the year Kindle was introduced, it is a perfect example of remediation and nostalgia.[5] Nostalgia locates one *in* time and through awareness *of* time passing; it is "a symptom of our age, a historical emotion." The paper email notepad stopped me in my tracks in 2007 in ways that it would *not* today. It is now just part of post-digital culture—a culture that, in 2007, I did not fully understand or even recognize I was part of. Recognizing this fact—how quickly things change in our digital world—should foreground the need to slow down and try to understand it.

What my study has taught me is both the value and the complexity of close reading, that central and traditional practice of literary criticism that privileges slow, careful reading and rereading. Close reading, as I contend and hope that I have modeled throughout my chapters, has never been so important, even as it also needs to adapt so that it can operate in other modes and with other objects than English departments have sometimes recognized. We need to attend carefully to the relationship between form and content but also to the relationship between format and networked media. Such attention is necessary for explaining a world in which the literary is not limited to text or contained in books but spread widely across the digital network. In a world of digital data, speed reading, and fake news, wherein Silicon Valley valorizes disruption over tradition, contemplation and critique are dissuaded. Analytical skills such as close reading and historicization taught through literature and literary studies are not antithetical to the digital moment, nor do they need to be threatened by it; they have always developed alongside the social practices of mediated life, and they are vital practices for living in our contemporary moment.

My experience with the paper email notepad is also a reminder of the power of objects. The little notepad nudged me toward this study of bookishness and also became a symbol of it—a fetish and memorial that accompanied me throughout the decade I took to complete this book. My relationship to the paper notepad exemplifies what the feminist philosopher Sara Ahmed calls "stickiness," a powerful but ambiguous affective force that draws us to objects and the hidden "histories of contact" they possess.[6] By taking seriously objects of bookishness and the stickiness factor that binds them to us, I have tried to introduce a new conceptual paradigm through which to understand the contemporary. Bookishness is the sticky factor that binds the contemporary literary into a formative feature of the twenty-first century.[7]

NOTES

INTRODUCTION

1. On simulacra, see Jean Baudrillard, *Simulations*, trans. Paul Foss, Paul Patton, and Philip Beitchman (New York: Semiotext(e), 1983).
2. Raymond Williams, *Marxism and Literature* (Oxford: Oxford University Press, 1997), 122.
3. Charles Acland follows Raymond Williams in framing his collection *Residual Media*, and the essays it contains on medial shift, as "a study of the aging of culture, asserting that the introduction of new cultural phenomena and material rests on an encounter with existing forms and practices. The result is both material accumulation and ever more elaborate modes of accommodation" (xx). Charles Acland, introduction to *Residual Media*, ed. Charles Acland (Minneapolis: University of Minnesota Press, 2007).
4. David Revere McFadden, *Slash: Paper Under the Knife* (New York: Museum of Arts and Design, 2009), 11, 14.
5. Pamela Paulsrud, *Touchstones*, 2013, https://pamelapaulsrud.com /artwork/197502_Touchstones.html; Brian Dettmer, *New Funk Standards*, 2017 (hardcover book, acrylic varnish. 12 ¾ × 12 × 5 ¾" [32.4 × 30.5 × 14.6 cm]), Nancy Toomey Fine Art, https://www.artsy.net /artwork/brian-dettmer-new-funk-standards.
6. Garrett Stewart, *Bookwork: Medium to Object to Concept to Art* (Chicago: University of Chicago Press, 2011).

7. For more on how Jane Austen has been used to sell commodities, including soap for Lever Brothers in the late nineteenth century, see Janine Barchas, "Sense, Sensibility, and Soap: An Unexpected Case Study in Digital Resources for Book History," *Book History* 16 (2013): 185–214.

8. See, for example, Ann Foster, "10 Great Pride and Prejudice Retellings for All Ages," BootRiot.com, April 30, 2018, https://bookriot.com/2018/04/30/pride-and-prejudice-retellings/.

9. Lisa Occhipinti, *The Repurposed Library: 33 Craft Projects That Give Old Books New Life* (New York: Abrams, 2011), 6–7.

10. Lane Smith, *It's a Book* (New York: Roaring Brook, 2010).

11. Hervé Tullet, *Press Here* (San Francisco: Chronicle, 2011).

12. See Naomi Baron, *Always On: Language in an Online and Mobile World* (Oxford: Oxford University Press, 2010).

13. Though there were earlier attempts at introducing digital reading devices to the general public, it was only after Sony's Reader in 2004 that Kindle and Nook took off (in 2007 and 2009, respectively) and changed everything. For a brief introduction to the long and ambiguous history of the "first" e-reader, see Alison Flood, "Where Did the Story of Ebooks Begin?," *Guardian*, March 12, 2014, https://www.theguardian.com/books/2014/mar/12/ebooks-begin-medium-reading-peter-james.

14. Motoko Rich, "Literacy Debate: Online, R U Really Reading?," *New York Times*, July 7, 2008, https://www.nytimes.com/2008/07/27/books/27reading.html.

15. Julie Bosman, "Times Will Rank E-book Best Sellers," *New York Times*, November 11, 2010, http://www.nytimes.com/2010/11/11/books/11list.html.

16. See Chris Anderson and Michael Wolff, "The Web Is Dead, Long Live the Internet," *Wired*, August, 17, 2010, https://www.wired.com/2010/08/ff_webrip/, which begins, "As much as we love the open, unfettered Web, we're abandoning it for simpler, sleeker services that just work."

17. Jonathan Segura, "Print Book Sales Rose Again in 2016," *Publisher's Weekly*, January 6, 2017, https://www.publishersweekly.com/pw/by-topic/industry-news/bookselling/article/72450-print-book-sales-rose-again-in-2016.html.

18. N. Katherine Hayles, *Electronic Literature: New Horizons for the Literary* (South Bend, IN: Notre Dame University Press, 2008), 159. With

"textual condition," Hayles references Jerome McGann's seminal *The Textual Condition* (Princeton, NJ: Princeton University Press, 1991), a work that greatly informs my own.

19. Or for readers interested in new media studies, think of how Henry Jenkins's concept of "convergence culture," which, he carefully explained in 2006, is now just a fact of life. "Participatory culture" and "prosumption," terms that Jenkins used to explain the then-emerging technocultural world of the early 2000s, is now just "culture." Henry Jenkins, *Convergence Culture: Where Old and New Media Collide* (New York: NYU Press, 2006).

20. Amazon.com is just behind Apple and Microsoft, according to "The Top 100 Best Performing Companies in the World, 2019," *CEOWorld*, June 28, 2019, https://ceoworld.biz/2019/06/28/the-top-100-best-performing-companies-in-the-world-2019/.

21. Mark McGurl, "Everything and Less: Fiction in the Age of Amazon," *Modern Language Quarterly* 77, no. 30 (September 2016): 447.

22. Marshall McLuhan and Quentin Fiore, *The Medium Is the Massage: An Inventory of Effects* (New York: Bantam, 1967), 10.

23. On media-specific analysis see N. Katherine Hayles, *Writing Machines*, Mediaworks Pamphlet Series (Cambridge, MA: MIT Press, 2002), esp. chap. 2. On media archaeology, see Erkki Huhtamo and Jussi Parikka, eds., *Media Archaeology: Approaches, Applications, and Implications* (Berkeley: University of California Press, 2011).

24. Craig Dworkin, *No Medium* (Cambridge, MA: MIT Press, 2013), 30.

25. David Thorburn and Henry Jenkins, "Introduction: Toward an Aesthetics of Transition," in *Rethinking Media Change: The Aesthetics of Transition*, ed. David Thorburn and Henry Jenkins (Cambridge, MA: MIT Press, 2003), 11.

26. Rita Felski, *The Limits of Critique* (Chicago: University of Chicago Press, 2015), 165.

27. Rita Felski, *Uses of Literature* (Oxford: Blackwell, 2008), 21.

28. Deidre Shauna Lynch, *Loving Literature: A Cultural History* (Chicago: University of Chicago Press, 2015), 165.

1. HOW AND NOW BOOKISHNESS

1. Victor Hugo, *The Hunchback of Notre Dame* (1831), book 5, chap. 1.

2. Qtd. in Ann M. Blair, *Too Much to Know: Managing Scholarly Information Before the Modern Age* (New Haven, CT: Yale University Press, 2010), 55.

3. See Elizabeth Eisenstein, *The Printing Press as an Agent of Change* (Cambridge: Cambridge University Press, 1980).

4. Leah Price, "Dead Again," *New York Times Book Review*, August 10, 2012, http://www.nytimes.com/2012/08/12/books/review/the-death-of-the-book-through-the-ages.html. Also see her recent book, *What We Talk About When We Talk About Books* (New York: Basic Books, 2019).

5. Priscilla Coit Murphy identifies three theories that constitute writing about the death of the book: that "media are rivals of each other," that "a new medium so affects an existing one that the two converge to meet all prior purposes and perhaps a few new ones," and that "new media—following a period of shifting and settling—are thought to take on complementary functions with respect to other media." See Priscilla Coit Murphy, "Books Are Dead, Long Live Books," in *Rethinking Media Change: The Aesthetics of Transition*, ed. David Thornburn and Henry Jenkins (Cambridge, MA: MIT Press, 2003): 90–91. The death of the book genre is what the media scholar Erkki Huhtamo describes as a cultural topos, a central feature of media archaeology: "Cultural desires are expressed by being embedded them within topoi." Erkki Huhtamo, "Dismantling the Fairy Engine: Media Archaeology as Topos Study," in *Media Archaeology: Approaches, Applications, and Implications*, ed. Erkki Huhtamo and Jussi Parikka (Berkeley: University of California Press, 2011), 28.

6. Nicolas Carr's essay caught like wildfire and became the cornerstone of his book *The Shallows: What the Internet Is Doing to Our Brains* (New York: Norton, 2010).

7. Sven Birkets, *The Gutenberg Elegies: The Fate of Reading in the Electronic Age* (New York: Faber and Faber, 1994), 228.

8. Nicolas Carr, "Is Google Making Us Stupid?" *The Atlantic*, July/August 2008, https://www.theatlantic.com/magazine/archive/2008/07/is-google-making-us-stupid/306868/.

9. See Frederic Jameson, *The Political Unconscious: Narrative as a Socially Symbolic Act* (Ithaca, NY: Cornell University Press, 1981).

10. Ted Striphas smartly states, "In the end, claims about the decline of books and book culture probably tells [*sic*] us more about the gaps in book history that need filling or about popular culture's proclivities toward crisis discourse than it does about the health of books in the

twentieth and twenty-first centuries." Ted Striphas, *The Late Age of Print: Everyday Book Culture from Consumerism to Control* (New York: Columbia University Press, 2009), 188.

11. Leah Price, *How to Do Things with Books in Victorian England* (Princeton, NJ: Princeton University Press, 2012).

12. Deidre Shauna Lynch, "Canons' Clockwork: Novels for Everyday Use," in *Bookish Histories: Books, Literature, and Commercial Modernity, 1700–1900*, ed. Ina Ferris and Paul Keen (London: Palgrave MacMillan, 2009), 90.

13. Peter Stallybrass argues, "To imagine continuous reading as the norm in reading a book is radically reactionary: it is to read a codex as if it was a scroll, from beginning to end." Peter Stallybrass, "Books and Scrolls: Navigating the Bible," in *Books and Readers in Early Modern England*, ed. Jennifer Andersen and Elizabeth Saur (State College: University of Pennsylvania Press, 2002), 48.

14. "As cultivated by the nineteenth-century novel, cover-to-cover escapism of this sort is an anomaly in the long history of reading." Matthew Brown, "Undisciplined Reading: Finding Surprise in How We Read," *Common-Place* 8, no. 1 (October 2007), http://common-place.org/book/undisciplined-reading/.

15. See Lisa Gitelman, *Paper Knowledge: Toward a Media History of Documents* (Durham, NC: Duke University Press, 2014).

16. National Endowment for the Arts, "Reading at Risk: A Survey of Literary Reading in America," June 2004, https://www.arts.gov/publications/reading-risk-survey-literary-reading-america-0.

17. Dana Gioia, preface to "Reading at Risk," National Endowment for the Arts, vii.

18. See Geoffrey Nunberg, "In Unread America," commentary for *Fresh Air*, December 8, 2004, http://people.ischool.berkeley.edu/~nunberg/curling.html. Nunberg provides a short history of the phrase "curling up with a good book," which is, of course, fraught with gendered and class connotations.

19. Matthew Kirschenbaum, "Reading at Risk: A Response," MGK: Matthew G. Kirschenbaum's Blog, July 21, 2004.

20. Simone Murray, *The Digital Literary Sphere: Reading, Writing, and Selling Books in the Internet Era* (Baltimore, MD: Johns Hopkins University Press, 2018), 140.

21. On these changes, see Price, *What We Talk About When We Talk About Books*, where she writes, "When we mourn the book, we're really mourning the death of those in-between moments (waiting in line, riding a bus)" (8). Also see Jason Farman's examination of waiting as a lost art in a digital age, *Delayed Response: The Art of Waiting from the Ancient to the Instant World* (New Haven, CT: Yale University Press, 2018): "Our time is calibrated to a notion of efficiency that, in a single gesture, both demonizes waiting and preys on it as the opportune moment to occupy our attention" (16).

22. Here I am thinking of Michel Foucault's work illuminating the discursive tools used for governmental and societal control, of which the book is certainly one. For example, see *The Archaeology of Knowledge and The Discourse on Language*, trans. A. M. Sheridan Smith (1969; New York: Pantheon, 1972).

23. Price, *What We Talk About When We Talk About Books*, 3.

24. Garrett Stewart, *Bookwork: Medium to Object to Concept to Art* (Chicago: University of Chicago Press, 2010), 67.

25. Florian Brody, "The Medium Is the Memory," in *The Digital Dialectic: New Essays on New Media*, ed. Peter Lunenfeld (Cambridge, MA: MIT Press, 1999), 135.

26. Patricia Crain has identified "a codicology of the modern self" emerging through book-based synecdoche in early American children's primers. "These two notions of bookness, as they relate to the codex form, are long-lived: the book as a sacred or quasi-sacred object and the book as a container for something that one must go to the book to acquire in order to fill the heart—or, in a sense, to have a heart at all, to become, that is, a self" (155). Patricia Crain, "Reading Childishly? A Codicology of the Modern Self," in *Comparative Textual Media: Transforming the Humanities in the Postprint Era*, ed. N. Katherine Hayles and Jessica Pressman (Minneapolis: University of Minnesota Press, 2013).

27. Scholarship on the relationship between books and hegemonic cultural values (Western, white, male, and class privilege) is long and varied, from D. F. McKenzie's classic *The Sociology of a Text: Oral Culture, Literacy, and Print in Early New Zealand: The Treaty of Waitang* (Wellington: Victoria University Press, 1985) to work on the history of the novel as a genre reflecting bourgeois identity and values, such as

Michael McKeon, *The Origins of the English Novel, 1600–1740* (Baltimore, MD: Johns Hopkins University Press, 1987).

28. Lucien Febvre and Henri-Jean Martin, *The Coming of the Book: The Impact of Printing, 1450–1800*, trans. David Gerard (1958, 1976; New York: Verso, 2000), 11.

29. See Stallybrass, "Books and Scrolls," 42–79.

30. "In an era in which even digital album sales have fallen, vinyl has bucked the trend. In 2014, record sales grew by more than 50% to hit more than a million, the highest since 1996—and the upward curve has continued in 2015." Lee Barron, "Why Vinyl Has Made a Comeback," *Newsweek*, April 18, 2015.

31. For example, John Locke and Sigmund Freud both describe, and thereby inscribe, an understanding of cognition (Locke) and consciousness (Freud) into Western thought through bookish metaphors: Locke's concept of the human mind as a blank slate or white page open to education and Freud's image of the mystic writing pad.

32. Ralph Waldo Emerson, "The American Scholar," in *Emerson: Essays and Poems*, 1st college ed. (New York: Library of America, 1996), 57.

33. See Kate Flint, *The Woman Reader, 1837–1914* (New York: Oxford University Press, 1993).

34. Bonnie Mak, *How the Book Matters* (Toronto: University of Toronto Press, 2011), 47.

35. Mak, *How the Book Matters*, 53.

36. Joanne Kaufman, "With Kindle, Can You Tell It's Proust?," *New York Times*, April 24, 2009.

37. Talib Choudhry, "The Rise of the Shelfie: How Good Looking Is Your Book Case?," *Telegraph*, February 2, 2017.

38. The Australian artist Victoria Reichelt remediates the shelfie by backward-designing it into painted portraits of people based on their bookshelves; see her *Bibliomania: The Bookshelf Portrait Project* (2008), http://www.victoriareichelt.com/. The literary scholar Garrett Stewart traces the history of a genre of portraiture that could be the elder sibling to the contemporary shelfie: paintings of individuals immersed in reading books, which he identifies as "the scene of reading." Garrett Stewart, *The Look of Reading: Book, Painting, Text* (Chicago: University of Chicago Press, 2006).

39. See Jay David Bolter and Richard Grusin, *Remediation: Understanding New Media* (Cambridge, MA: MIT Press, 1999); and N. Katherine Hayles, "Intermediation: From Page to Screen," in *Electronic Literature: New Horizons for the Literary* (South Bend, IN: Notre Dame University Press, 2008), which updates the concept of "remediation."
40. Henry Petroski, *The Book on the Bookshelf* (New York: Vintage, 1999), 94.
41. See Johanna Drucker, "The Virtual Codex from Page Space to E-Space," in *A Companion to Digital Literary Studies*, ed. R. Siemens and S. Schreibman (Wiley-Blackwell, 2013), doi:10.1002/9781405177504.ch11.
42. On "skeuomorph," see N. Katherine Hayles, *How We Became Posthuman: Virtual Bodies in Cybernetics, Literature, and Informatics* (Chicago: University of Chicago Press, 1999), esp. chap. 1.
43. Andrew Piper, *Book Was There: Reading in Electronic Times* (Chicago: University of Chicago Press, 2012), 26. Henry Sussman, *Around the Book: Systems and Literacy* (Fordham University Press, 2011), 2, similarly suggests, "There is something irreducibly tactile in our relation to the book"; "It confronts us at eye-level. It addresses us face-to-face."
44. Piper, *Book Was There*, ix.

2. SHELTER

1. Jennifer Egan, *The Keep* (New York: Knopf, 2006), 47.
2. Egan, *The Keep*, 40, 26.
3. Egan, *The Keep*, 246.
4. Egan, *The Keep*, 255, 254.
5. Jess Walter, *The Zero* (New York: HarperCollins, 2006), 3.
6. Walter, *The Zero*, 306, 9, 97.
7. Walter, *The Zero*, 97, 19.
8. See Marshall McLuhan, *The Gutenberg Galaxy: The Making of Typographic Man* (Toronto: University of Toronto Press, 1962), 91.
9. Jonathan Safran Foer, *Extremely Loud & Incredibly Close* (New York: Houghton Mifflin Harcourt, 2005), 325.
10. I want to take the space of the page to express gratitude to my friend and former colleague Sam See, who suggested this passage in Foer's novel as an example of bookishness at this project's very early stages. He was a dear friend, and I miss him.

11. Safran Foer, *Extremely Loud & Incredibly Close*, 325.

12. Richard Drew, *Time Magazine*, http://100photos.time.com/photos /richard-drew-falling-man.

13. William Joyce, *The Fantastic Flying Books of Mr. Morris Lessmore* (New York: Simon & Schuster, 2012). There are no page numbers in the volume.

14. Sara Tanderup, "Touching Books on Screen: Bridging Media Cultures and Generations with William Joyce's *The Fantastic Flying Books of Mr. Morris Lessmore*," *Paradoxa: Studies in World Literary Genres* 29, special ed., "Small Screen Fictions," ed. Astrid Ensslin, Lisa Swanstrom, and Pawel Frelik (2018): 28.

15. Ture Schwebs, "Affordances of an App: A Reading of *The Fantastic Flying Books of Mr. Morris Lessmore*," *Nordic Journal of Child Lit* 5, no. 1 (2014), https://doi.org/10.3402/blft.v5.24169.

16. On the history of American primers teaching young readers to see themselves in books and identify as bookish, see Patricia Crain, *The Story of A: The Alphabetization of America from* The New England Primer *to* The Scarlet Letter (Stanford, CA: Stanford University Press, 2000).

17. Andrew Piper, *Book Was There: Reading in Electronic Times* (Chicago: University of Chicago Press, 2012): 26.

18. Robin Sloane, *Mr. Penumbra's 24-Hour Bookstore* (New York: Farrar, Straus and Giroux, 2012), 136.

19. Regis Debray writes, "A receptacle of the Revelation . . . the container benefited over the long run from the contents' sacredness, such that 'to believe in the Book' and to believe in God gradually became synonymous" (141). See "The Book as Symbolic Object," in *The Future of the Book*, ed. Geoffrey Nunberg (Berkeley: University of California Press, 1996), 139–51.

20. Siva Vaidhyanathan, *The Googlization of Everything (and Why We Should Worry)* (Berkeley: University of California Press, 2011), 4.

21. Sloane, *Mr. Penumbra's 24-Hour Bookstore*, 274–75.

22. On media-specific analysis, see N. Katherine Hayles, *Writing Machines* (Cambridge, MA: MIT Press, 2002). On Marshall McLuhan's key phrase "the medium is the message," see *Understanding Media: The Extensions of Man* (Cambridge, MA: MIT Press, 1964).

23. See Safiya Umoja Noble, *Algorithms of Oppression: How Search Engines Reinforce Racism* (New York: NYU Press, 2018).

24. I want to thank my friend and colleague Mike Borgstrom for pushing me to consider this question and many others.

25. Kathleen Fitzpatrick, *The Anxiety of Obsolescence: The American Novel in the Age of Television* (Nashville, TN: Vanderbilt University Press, 2006), 17, 5.

26. Carla Hesse, "Books in Time," in *The Future of the Book*, ed. Geoffrey Nunberg (Berkeley: University of California Press, 1996), 27.

27. Christina Lupton, *Reading and the Making of Time in the Eighteenth Century* (Baltimore, MD: Johns Hopkins University Press, 2018), 23.

28. "Playbor" is a portmanteau of "play" and "labor" and refers to the type of free labor that gamers and users of the Web do, often willingly and unknowingly. "These are new forms of labor but old forms of exploitation," as Trebor Scholz writes in his introduction to *Digital Labor: The Internet as Playground and Factory*, ed. Trebor Scholz (New York: Routledge, 2013), 1.

29. The origins of the slow-food movement are attributed to a 1986 protest against the opening of a McDonald's in Rome. Also see Maggie Berg and Barbara K. Seeber, *The Slow Professor: Challenging the Culture of Speed in the Academy* (Toronto: University of Toronto Press, 2016).

30. Matthew Jenkin, "Tablets Out, Imagination In: The Schools That Shun Technology," *Guardian*, December 2, 2015, https://www.theguardian.com/teachernetwork/2015/dec/02/schools-that-ban-tablets-traditional-education-silicon-valleylondon.

31. Theodor H. Nelson, *Computer Lib/Dream Machines* (Redmond, WA: Tempus Books of Microsoft Press, 1987).

3. THING

1. "The codex as a technology of discontinuity made at first possible and finally easy the collation of the Pentateuch, the Prophets, the Gospels, the Epistles, and the Psalms on a daily basis." Peter Stallybrass, "Books and Scrolls: Navigating the Bible," in *Books and Readers in Early Modern England*, ed. Jennifer Andersen and Elizabeth Saur (Philadelphia: University of Pennsylvania Press, 2002), 73.

2. Régis Debray, "The Book as Symbolic Object," in *The Future of the Book*, ed. Geoffrey Nunberg (Berkeley: University of California Press, 1996), 142. "The dogma of the Incarnation and the belief in the resurrection

of bodies predisposed one to consider sacred the body of the Book, Spirit made object, Word became papyrus or parchment. An author's soul made flesh" (142).

3. Bonnie Mak, *How the Page Matters* (Toronto: University of Toronto Press, 2011), 3.

4. Anne Fadiman, *Ex Libris: Confessions of a Common Reader* (New York: Farrar, Straus and Giroux, 1998), xi.

5. Andrew Piper, *Book Was There: Reading in Electronic Times* (Chicago: University of Chicago Press, 2012), xi.

6. William Pietz, "The Problem of the Fetish, II: The Origin of the Fetish," *RES: Anthropology and Aesthetics* 9 (Spring 1985): 5.

7. For a history of the fetish concept, see Pietz, "The Problem of the Fetish," 5: "The fetish, as an idea and a problem, and as a novel object not proper to any prior discrete society, originated in the cross-cultural spaces of the coast of West Africa during the sixteenth and seventeenth centuries." Hartmut Böhme contends that "fetishism was above all a European phenomenon," a specifically nineteenth-century means of negotiating a "thingly environment—to collecting, trading, hoarding." Hartmut Böhme, *Fetishism and Culture: A Different Theory of Modernity*, trans. Anna Galt (Berlin: De Gruyter, 2014), 187, 5.

8. Pietz, "The Problem of the Fetish," 7.

9. Sigmund Freud understood fetishism as a result of trauma and loss. In "Fetishism" (1927), in *Sexuality and the Psychology of Love* (New York: Touchstone, 1997), he explains that the original lack, the mother's lack of a penis, registers for a boy a "horror of castration [that] sets up a sort of permanent memorial to itself by creating this substitute" (206). This metonymic substitution results in a fetish that is both a signifier and archive of that which was lost. As a result, the fetish object also staves off future loss. Freud writes, "the purpose of the fetish precisely is to preserve it from being lost" (205). Objects of bookishness function, in psychoanalytic terms, to help us move beyond mourning the presumed loss of books in a digital age. We might consider films like *The Joy of Books* and other forms of bookishness as operating like a transitional object. See D. W. Winnicott, "Transitional Objects and Transitional Phenomena—a Study of the First Not-Me Possession," *International Journal of Psycho-Analysis* 34 (1953): 89–97.

10. Nicolas Hudson, "It-Narratives: Fictional Point of View and Constructing the Middle Class," in *The Secret Life of Things: Animals, Objects, and It-Narratives in Eighteenth-Century England*, ed. Mark Blackwell (Lewisburg, PA: Bucknell University Press, 2007).

11. Leah Price, *How to Do Things with Books in Victorian England* (Princeton, NJ: Princeton University Press, 2012), 110.

12. What these scholarly conversations share is an attempt to grapple with how "new ways of thinking about living matter are radically and rapidly reconfiguring our material world— both empirically and conceptually." When bioengineering can produce living matter in a test tube and medical technology can keep a body alive long after the brain has died, the question of what counts as life is up for grabs. In this world (our world), the question of what distinguishes animate from inanimate is a heated topic, which is why we see a renewed attention to objects. On new materialism, see Diana Coole and Samantha Frost, eds., *New Materialisms: Ontology, Agency, and Politics* (Chapel Hill, NC: Duke University Press, 2010). On object-oriented ontology, see Graham Harman, *Towards Speculative Realism: Essays and Lecture* (New York: Zero, 2010); and Ian Bogost, *Alien Phenomenology; or, What It's Like to Be a Thing* (Minneapolis: University of Minnesota Press, 2012). On actor-network theory, see Bruno Latour, *Reassembling the Social: An Introduction to Actor-Network-Theory* (Oxford: Oxford University Press, 2005).

13. Patrick Jagoda, *Network Aesthetics* (Chicago: University of Chicago Press, 2016), 185.

14. Carlos María Domínguez, *The House of Paper*, trans. Nick Castor (New York: Harcourt, 2005), 1–2.

15. María Domínguez, *The House of Paper*, 6, 8, 9.

16. María Domínguez, *The House of Paper*, 9.

17. María Domínguez, *The House of Paper*, 54, 70, 84.

18. Amaranth Borsuk and Brad Bouse, *Between Page and Screen* (Siglio, 2012). Unlike full-blown virtual reality, wherein a user dons a headset in order to have a completely immersive virtual experience, augmented reality uses data markers such as QR (quick response) codes and computational scanning devices to supplement real life and project layers of content into a real space.

19. Here I am cribbing the frontispiece text of Mark Z. Danielewski's *House of Leaves* (New York: Pantheon, 2000): "This is not for you."

20. This is not, for instance, the "look of reading" that Garret Stewart catalogs in his book by that title: *The Look of Reading: Book, Painting, Text* (Chicago: University of Chicago Press, 2006).

21. For more on the implications of this point and a close reading of *Between Page and Screen* in relation to issues of translation and the field of comparative literature, see Jessica Pressman, "Re-Orienting Ourselves Towards the Material: *Between Page and Screen* as Case Study," *Comparative Literature* 70, no. 3 (September 2018).

22. *Between Page and Screen* narrativizes Mak's point in *How the Page Matters* that to claim that the page matters means "not only [for the page] to be of importance, to signify, to mean, but also to claim a certain physical space, to have a particular presence, to be uniquely embodied" (3).

23. The first stop-motion film by the creators of *The Joy of Books*, Sean and Lisa Ohlenkamp, was titled *Organizing the Bookcase* (2011) and focused on this one aspect: moving books around on a bookshelf. https://youtu.be/zhRT-PM7vpA.

24. https://www.youtube.com/watch?v=SKVcQnyEIT8.

25. Charlie White, "Remarkable 'Joy of Books' Animation Brings Books to Life," *Mashable*, January 29, 2012, http://mashable.com/2012/01/29/joy-of-books-viralvideo/#enW6FT77BGqI.

26. http://theinspirationroom.com/daily/2009/new-zealand-book-council-going-west/.

27. https://vimeo.com/2295261.

28. https://vimeo.com/31005042.

29. Charles Musser, *The Emergence of Cinema: The American Screen to 1907* (Berkeley: University of California Press, 1994).

30. See the exhibition dedicated to Tim Burton at New York City's Museum of Modern Art (November 22, 2009–April 26, 2010), which describes Burton as having "reinvented Hollywood genre filmmaking." https://www.moma.org/calendar/exhibitions/313.

31. The statement is the perfect articulation of commodity fetishism. It is addressed to you, the viewer, and invites you to enter the fantasy through ownership. For an expanded reading of this part of the film, see Jessica Pressman, " 'There's Nothing Quite Like a Real Book': Stop-Motion Bookishness," in *The Printed Book in Contemporary American Culture: Medium, Object, Metaphor*, ed. Heike Schaefer and Alexander Starre (New York: Palgrave Macmillan, 2019).

32. It is relevant for understanding the capitalist forces shaping bookish relationships to know that YouTube, where *The Joy of Books* is hosted, was purchased by Google in 2006.

33. The video was shot at Toronto's Type Books, and when asked why he selected that particular location for filming, Sean Ohlenkamp responded, "They're an independent brick-and-mortar store and when you're talking about real books, they add a level of creativity, charm and a human touch to it all." Qtd. in Melody Lau, "Q&A: Sean Ohlenkamp, the Man Behind Type's Viral 'Joy of Books' Video," *National Post*, January 10, 2012, http://nationalpost.com/afterword/qa -sean-ohlenkamp-the-man-behind-typesviral-joy-of-books-video.

34. See Simone Murray, *The Digital Literary Sphere: Reading, Writing, and Selling Books in the Internet Era* (Baltimore, MD: Johns Hopkins University Press, 2018).

35. Leanne Shapton, *Important Artifacts and Personal Property from the Collection of Lenore Doolan and Harold Morris, Including Books, Street Fashion, and Jewelry* (Sarah Crichton Books; New York: Farrar, Straus and Giroux, 2009), 4.

36. Shapton, *Important Artifacts*, 78–79.

37. Shapton, *Important Artifacts*, 67.

38. Maurizia Boscagli, *Stuff Theory: Everyday Objects, Radical Materialism* (New York: Bloomsbury, 2014), 6.

39. Susan Stewart, *On Longing: Narratives of the Miniature, the Gigantic, the Souvenir, the Collection* (Baltimore, MD: Johns Hopkins University Press, 1984), 135.

4. FAKE

1. Demeter Fragrance Library, https://demeterfragrance.com/paperback .html; Paper Passion Perfume, https://steidl.de/Books/Paper-Passion -Perfume-0008152458.html.

2. Walter Benjamin, "The Work of Art in the Age of Mechanical Reproduction" (1936), in *Illuminations*, trans. Harry Zohn, ed. Hannah Arendt (New York: Schocken/Random House, 1969): 217–51.

3. See A. M. Turing, "On Computable Numbers, with an Application to the Entscheidungsproblem," *Proceedings of the London Mathematical Society* s2-42, no. 1 (1937): 241.

4. Steven Johnson, *Interface Culture: How New Technology Transforms the Way We Create and Communicate* (New York: Basic Books, 1997), 15.

5. Kati Stevens, *Fake* (New York: Bloomsbury Academic, 2019), 6.

6. See Jean Baudrillard, *Simulations*, trans. Paul Foss, Paul Patton, and Philip Beitchman (Brooklyn: Semiotext(e), 1983).

7. On "dummy spines," see Rowan Watson, "Some Non-Textual Uses of Books," in *A Companion to the History of the Book*, ed. Simon Eliot and Jonathan Rose (Oxford: Blackwell, 2007), 480–92. Watson discusses dummy spines back to the early eighteenth century. Also see Leah Price, "The Subconscious Shelf," *New York Times Sunday Book Review*, November 10, 2011, https://www.nytimes.com/2011/11/13/books /review/the-subconscious-shelf.html. The relationship between literary criticism and fakery is deeply bound; early literary forgeries helped promote the emergence of literary criticism as a field of study, as the possibility that a literary artifact might be a fake prompted the emergence of philology and textual studies as practices to determine the authorial identity and trace the bibliographic histories of textual artifacts. See K. K. Ruthven, *Faking Literature* (Cambridge: Cambridge University Press, 2001); and Anthony Grafton, *Forgers and Critics: Creativity and Duplicity in Western Scholarship* (Princeton, NJ: Princeton University Press, 1990).

8. Mindell Dubanksy, *Blooks: The Art of Books That Aren't: Book Objects from the Collection of Mindell Dubansky* (New York: Grolier Club, 2016), 6, 1. Dubanksy shows that some of the earliest blooks enclosed precious religious books dating back to the Middle Ages, though she notes a boom in American blooks in the late nineteenth century.

9. Holbrook Jackson, *The Anatomy of Bibliomania* (New York: Farrar, Straus and Company, 1950), 135.

10. Rowan Watson, "Some Non-Textual Uses of Books," 490. The information on Bernays is from Larry Tye, *The Father of Spin: Edward L. Bernays and the Birth of Public Relations* (New York: Picador, 1998), esp. 52. Also see Ted Striphas, *The Late Age of Print: Everyday Book Culture from Consumerism to Control* (New York: Columbia University Press, 2009), 27–30.

11. https://www.target.com/p/hepburn-quote-decorative-book-set-of-3 /-/A-50903472.

12. Stevens, *Fake*, 10.

13. https://society6.com/product/vintage-mr-darcy-proposal-from
-pride-and-prejudice-byjane-austen_leggings.
14. Stevens, *Fake*, 63.
15. "The most significant aspect of review culture as it manifests in the
digital literary sphere is its greatly broadened base of participation."
Simone Murray, *The Digital Literary Sphere: Reading, Writing, and Selling
Books in the Internet Era* (Baltimore, MD: Johns Hopkins University
Press, 2018), 118.
16. Norbert Elias, "*Kitsch* Style and the Age of *Kitsch* [1935]," in *Collected
Works of Norbert Elias*, vol. 1: *Early Writings* (Dublin: University of College Dublin Press, 2005), 87.
17. "Kitsch, technologically as well as aesthetically, is one of the most
typical products of modernity." Matei Calinescu, *Faces of Modernity:
Avant-Garde, Decadence, Kitsch* (Bloomington: Indiana University Press,
1977), 226. "Mechanical reproduction not only altered the proliferation and affordability of images, but also enabled a particular, modern sensibility based on the preeminence of looking and collecting."
Celeste Olalquiaga, *The Artificial Kingdom: A Treasury of the Kitsch Experience, with Remarkable Objects of Art and Nature, Extraordinary Events,
Eccentric Biography, and Original Theory, Plus Many Wonderful Illustrations
Selected by the Author* (New York: Pantheon, 1998), 13.
18. Hermann Broch, "Notes on the Problem of Kitsch," in *Kitsch: The World
of Bad Taste*, ed. Gillo Dorfles (New York: Bell, 1968), 73.
19. Daniel Tiffany, *My Silver Planet: A Secret History of Poetry and Kitsch* (Baltimore, MD: Johns Hopkins University Press, 2014), 3. In this book,
Tiffany locates the origins of kitsch not in the modern period but
instead in the eighteenth-century craze for literary hoaxes and false
antiquarianism, a time filled with tales of old manuscripts found in
trunks and the attribution of poems to fake poets.
20. J. J. Abrams and Doug Dorst, *S.* (New York: Mulholland Books, 2013), 396.
21. Canon Gate Books, https://canongate.co.uk/books/1748-s/.
22. Sianne Ngai, *Our Aesthetic Categories: Zany, Cute, Interesting* (Cambridge,
MA: Harvard University Press, 2012), 135.
23. Ngai, *Aesthetic Categories*, 135.
24. Qtd. in Logan Hill, "A Long Time Ago, in a Universe More Analog: J. J.
Abrams and Doug Dorst Collaborate on a Book, 'S.'" *New York Times*,
October 27, 2013, https://www.nytimes.com/2013/10/28/books/j

-jabrams-and-doug-dorst-collaborate-on-a-book-s.html. The literary scholar Amy Hungerford asserts a practice and politics of not reading, with David Foster Wallace as her case study, in *Making Literature Now* (Stanford, CA: Stanford University Press, 2016). I am not arguing that *S.* invites or deserves such a stance but that its payoff is physical presence rather than textual interpretation.

25. See the chapter "Markings," in Multigraph Collective, *Interacting with Print: Elements of Reading in the Era of Print Saturation* (Chicago: University of Chicago Press, 2017).

26. Abrams and Dorst, *S.*, 150.

27. Aaron Reed and Jacob Garbe, *The Ice-Bound Concordance*, app, 2016.

28. Aaron Reed and Jacob Garbe, *The Ice-Bound Compendium* (Simulacrum Liberation Press, 2016).

29. This is especially true of the bildungsroman genre. See Franco Moretti, *The Way of the World: The Bildungsroman in European Culture* (London: Verso, 1987).

30. The *New York Times* recently covered how Robin Sloane (whose novel, *Mr. Penumbra's 24-Hour Bookstore*, I discuss in chapter 2) is using an AI to assist him in writing his next novel. See David Streitfeld, "Computer Stories: A.I. Is Beginning to Assist Novelists," *New York Times*, October 18, 2018, https://www.nytimes.com/2018/10/18/technology/ai-is-beginning-to-assistnovelists.html.

31. On the role and importance of nonconscious cognizers in contemporary life, see N. Katherine Hayles, *Unthought: The Power of the Cognitive Nonconscious* (Chicago: University of Chicago Press, 2017).

5. WEAPON

1. See A. M. Turing, "On Computable Numbers, with an Application to the Entscheidungsproblem," *Proceedings of the London Mathematical Society* s2-42, no. 1 (1937).

2. N. Katherine Hayles, *How We Became Posthuman: Virtual Bodies in Cybernetics, Literature, and Informatics* (Chicago: University of Chicago Press, 1999).

3. See, for example, the anthology of criticism devoted to Danielewski's oeuvre, *Mark Z. Danielewski*, ed. Joe Bray and Alison Gibbons (Manchester: Manchester University Press, 2011).

4. For the purpose of clarity, or as much clarity as a chapter on such a complex novel will allow, I identify the film "The Navidson Record" with quotation marks and the manuscript *The Navidson Record* with italics.

5. Mark Z. Danielewski, *House of Leaves* (New York: Pantheon, 2000), xvii.

6. Danielewski, *House of Leaves*, 119.

7. The novel's cover claims that *House of Leaves* is published in four different editions: the Full Color edition ("house" is colored blue; "minotaur" and all struck passages are red), the 2-Color edition ("house" is colored blue), the Black & White edition, and the Incomplete edition. As far as I know, the Full Color and Incomplete editions do not exist. The 2-Color editions appear with either blue (for "house," minotaur and struck passages in black text) or red (for minotaur and struck passages, with "house" in light gray). The blue edition is supposedly the most prevalent in the United States.

8. Jessica Pressman, "*House of Leaves*: Reading the Networked Novel," *Studies in American Fiction* (2006): 107.

9. For example, I examine the pivotal and metarecursive scene near the end of the novel wherein Johnny Truant hears a band play "Five and a Half Minute Hallway," which is the title of the Navidson's short film, the discursive description of which Truant is editing from Zampanò's manuscript. The playing of that song by a band that has, diegetically, not yet read the manuscript triggers Truant's epiphany (and, of course, that of the novel's reader) that the narrative he edits extends beyond its pages. In this mind-bending moment, *House of Leaves* links up with a wider multimedia network beyond its bindings. The song "Five and a Half Minute Hallway" that Truant hears within the novel's diegetic narrative is also a song on Poe's album *Haunted*. Moreover, this song provides a clue to the question of authorship posited by Zampanò in the first lines of his narrative. See Pressman, "*House of Leaves*."

10. Pressman, "*House of Leaves*," 107–8.

11. This is true of the 2-Color edition but not of the Black & White edition; in that edition, "house" appears in the gray of grayscale tone.

12. Jay David Bolter and Richard Grusin, *Remediation: Understanding New Media* (Cambridge, MA: MIT Press, 1999), 15.

13. For more on Y2K and fears of the death of the book, see my discussion in chapter 1 of this book.

14. Danielewski, *House of Leaves*, xxiii.
15. Danielewski, *House of Leaves*, 3.
16. William J. Mitchell, *The Reconfigured Eye: Visual Truth in the Post-Photographic Era* (Cambridge, MA: MIT Press, 1992): 31.
17. Danielewski, *House of Leaves*, 30, 40 (emphasis added).
18. Jonathan Freedman, email to author, December 2008.
19. Hayles, *How We Became Posthuman*, 2.
20. Alan Liu, *Local Transcendence: Essays on Postmodern Historicism and the Database* (Chicago: University of Chicago Press, 2008), 220. Liu adapts the German media theorist Friedrich Kittler's famous concept of a "discourse network," a historical concept for designating cultural period based upon "the technologies and institutions that allow a given culture to select, store, and produce relevant data," and he identifies "discourse network 2000" as a contemporary new moment based upon the idea of Web 2.0. "These cardinal needs of transformability, autonomous mobility, and automation resolve at a more general level into what may be identified as the governing ideology of discourse network 2000: *the separation of content from material instantiation or formal presentation*" (216).
21. Steven Hall, *The Raw Shark Texts* (New York: Canongate, 2007), 3, 10, 18.
22. Hall, *The Raw Shark Texts*, 139, 141, 59.
23. Hall, *The Raw Shark Texts*, 61.
24. Miler Lagos, *Home*, for the Magnan Metz Gallery in New York City (September 12–October 15, 2011), http://www.magnanmetz.com/exhibitions/miler-lagos-home.
25. Hall, *The Raw Shark Texts*, 68.
26. On the relationship between new media and film, see Lev Manovich, *The Language of New Media* (Cambridge, MA: MIT Press, 2001). I examine how bookishness employs early cinematic techniques, specifically stop-motion filmmaking, in chapter 3.
27. Hall, *The Raw Shark Texts*, 63, 81.
28. Hall, *The Raw Shark Texts*, 265, 64.
29. "The new electronic interdependence recreates the world in the image of a global village." Marshall McLuhan, *The Gutenberg Galaxy: The Making of Typographic Man* (Toronto: University of Toronto Press, 1962), 43.

30. On the ideology of black boxes in computer software and ideologies surrounding it, see Wendy Hui Kyong Chun, *Programmed Visions: Software and Memory* (Cambridge, MA: MIT Press, 2011). The shift from DIY to distance is part of a longer history of configuring the computer's place in culture. See Fred Turner, *From Counterculture to Cyberculture: Stewart Brand, the Whole Earth Network, and the Rise of Digital Utopianism* (Chicago: University of Chicago Press, 2006), wherein he shows how "in the 1990s, the same machine that had served as the defining devices of cold war technology emerged as the symbols of its transformation" (2). The shift in the use and conception of what a computer was and could do was, namely, that "computers somehow seemed poised to bring to life the countercultural dream of empowered individualism, collaborative community, and spiritual communion" (2).

31. On the importance of the book's *thereness*, see Andrew Piper, *Book Was There: Reading in Electronic Times* (Chicago: University of Chicago Press, 2012).

32. For an extended close reading of *The Raw Shark Texts* as posthuman allegory, see Jessica Pressman, "The Aesthetic of Bookishness in 21st-Century Literature: Steven Hall's *The Raw Shark Texts*," *Michigan Quarterly Review* 48, no. 4 (Fall 2009).

33. See A. M. Turing, "Computing Machinery and Intelligence [1950]," in *The New Media Reader*, ed. Noah Wardrip-Fruin and Nick Monfort (Cambridge, MA: MIT Press, 2003), 200.

34. Alan Liu follows Wendell Piez in identifying John Hall's interchangeable part manufacturing process, introduced in the early nineteenth century and used at the U.S. armory at Harper's Ferry to build guns, as the predecessor to the logic of discourse network 2000. See Alan Liu, *Local Transcendence: Essays on Postmodern Historicism and the Database* (Chicago: University of Chicago Press, 2008).

35. Hall, *The Raw Shark Texts*, 202.

36. Computer viruses, Jussi Parikka reminds us, are not only products of technology and computation but also of capitalism: "Computer viruses can be conceived of as internal to the media ecology of digital capitalism." Jussi Parikka, *Digital Contagions: A Media Archaeology of Computer Viruses* (New York: Peter Lang, 2007), 5.

37. Matthew Kirschenbaum, *Track Changes: A History of Word Processing* (Cambridge, MA: Harvard University Press, 2016), argues that the "literary history of word processing," which includes tools like Microsoft Word and other word-processing software, exposes how these tools not only shape literary production but also "shapes and informs literary subjects" (xiii, 29).

38. Un-space resonates with the anthropologist Marc Augé's concept of "non-place," those ever-growing transitional "space[s] of supermodernity" that are not quite places (like airports and freeways) but where individuals share increasingly more time in our postmodern age. Marc Augé, *Non-Places: Introduction to an Anthropology of Supermodernity*, trans. John Howe (New York: Verso, 1995).

39. Hall, *The Raw Shark Texts*, 184, 227.

40. Hall, *The Raw Shark Texts*, 68.

6. MEMORIAL

1. Jonathan Safran Foer, "This Book and The Book," afterword to *Tree of Codes* (London: Visual Editions, 2010).

2. *The Street of Crocodiles* was originally published in Polish in 1934 as *Sklepy cynamonowe*, meaning "Cinnamon Shops," but was renamed when published in English in a translation by Celina Wieniewska in 1963. Foer cuts his title out of the translated publication. "Schulz experienced this [modernization] directly when oil was discovered in his native Drohobycz in 1901, turning the quiet provincial town into a 'wild Klondike.'" Colleen M. Taylor, "Childhood Revisited: The Writings of Bruno Schulz," *Slavic and East European Journal* 13, no. 4 (Winter 1969): 457. "The old dignity of the Cinnamon Shops, with their aroma of spices and distant countries, changed into something brash, second rate, questionable, slightly suspect." Celina Wieniewska, "Translator's Preface," in *The Complete Fiction of Bruno Schulz*, 1st ed. (New York: Walker & Company, 1989): x.

3. See Kiene Brillenburg Wurth, "Old and New Medialities in Foer's *Tree of Codes*," *Comparative Literature and Culture* 13, no. 3 (September 2011): 4, wherein she describes *Tree of Codes* as "the trace, the history of a reading."

4. Qtd. in Steven Heller, "Jonathan Safran Foer's Book as Art Object," *New York Times*, November 24, 2010, https://artsbeat.blogs.nytimes .com/2010/11/24/jonathan-safran-foersbook-as-art-object/.

5. Jerome J. McGann, *The Textual Condition* (Princeton, NJ: Princeton University Press, 1991).

6. In the Heideggerian sense, a page is a tool to-hand and ready for use if we know how to use it. *Tree of Codes* defamiliarizes the action of reading and turning a page and thus draws attention to the pageness and bookness of the very tools we use. Martin Heidegger, "The Question Concerning Technology," in *The Question Concerning Technology and Other Essays*, trans. William Lovitt (New York: Harper Torchbooks, 1977), 3–35.

7. Espen Aarseth, *Cybertext: Perspectives on Ergodic Literature* (Baltimore, MD: Johns Hopkins University Press, 1997), introduces the term "ergodic" (from the Greek *ergon* [work] and *hodos* [path]) to distinguish between works that require interaction to operate and those that do not. His taxonomy became the foundation for ludology or, later, game studies.

8. Aaron Mauro describes the geographically distributed network that produced the book in "Versioning Loss: Jonathan Safran Foer's *Tree of Codes* and the Materiality of Digital Publishing," *DHQ: Digital Humanities Quarterly* 8, no. 4 (2014): para. 4, http://www.digitalhumanities .org/dhq/vol/8/4/000192/000192.html.

9. Visual Editions, "Making *Tree of Codes*: 3 Months in 3 Minutes" (video), March 10, 2011, https://vimeo.com//20869635.

10. Hayles reminds us that all contemporary printed books are shaped in some way by digital production processes. N. Katherine Hayles, *My Mother Was a Computer: Digital Subjects and Literary Texts* (Chicago: University of Chicago Press, 2005).

11. Safran Foer, "This Book and The Book," 139.

12. Florian Cramer, "Post-Digital Writing," *electronic book review*, December 12, 2012, http://www.electronicbookreview.com/thread /electropoetics/postal; Florian Cramer, "What Is 'Post-Digital'?," *APRJA* 3, no. 1 (2014), http://www.aprja.net/what-is-post-digital/.

13. Safran Foer, *Tree of Codes*, 9, 8, 90–92, 91. Transcribing the content of the page into a linear format obviously transforms its meaning, but I attempt to denote the poetic presentation of text by using the

backslash to indicate a line break and the em-dash to denote the presence of a hole on the page.

14. Foer, *Tree of Codes*, 11.

15. Foer, *Tree of Codes*, 8, 9, 10, 100, 11, 13, 21.

16. Foer, *Tree of Codes*, 21, 67, 68, 73–75, 76.

17. "Like the human body, the book is a form of information transmission and storage, and like the human body, the book incorporates its encodings in a durable material substrate." N. Katherine Hayles, *How We Became Posthuman: Virtual Bodies in Cybernetics, Literature, and Informatics* (Chicago: University of Chicago Press, 1999), 28.

18. Paul Saenger, *Space Between Words: The Origins of Silent Reading* (Stanford, CA: Stanford University Press, 1997), 6.

19. "I have found that the whisper is the most salient metaphor to describe the experience of reading this book." Mauro, "Versioning Loss," para. 9.

20. N. Katherine Hayles, "Combining Close and Distant Reading: Jonathan Safran Foer's *Tree of Codes* and the Aesthetic of Bookishness," *PMLA*, 128, no. 1 (2013): 227.

21. Foer, *Tree of Codes*, 14–17.

22. The media theorist Friedrich Kittler identifies the mother as the central node in "discourse network 1800," arguing that around 1800 "the acquisition of language became the mother's prerogative" (31). Friedrich Kittler, *Discourse Networks 1800/1900*, trans. Michael Metteer with Chris Cullens (Stanford, CA: Stanford University Press, 1990).

23. Foer, *Tree of Codes*, 130–32.

24. Foer, *Tree of Codes*, 132–34.

25. Although it is often mentioned in surveys of contemporary digitally inflected literature, few scholars actually engage *Tree of Codes* in a serious interpretative manner. Kiene Brillenburg Wurth and N. Katherine Hayles are exceptions, with Wurth ("Old and New Medialities in Foer's *Tree of Codes*") pursuing an intermedial reading of the work and Hayles ("Combining Close and Distant Reading") approaching *Tree of Codes* through new kinds of computer-assisted reading practices.

26. Michel Faber, "*Tree of Codes* by Jonathan Safran Foer—Review," *Guardian*, December 17, 2010. Boris Kachka writes of *Tree of Codes*: "Inventive, for sure, but verging on Gimmicks 101." Boris Kachka, "Reinventing the Book: Jonathan Safran Foer's Object of Anti-Technology,"

New York Magazine, November 21, 2010, https://nymag.com/arts/books/features/69635/.

27. The intermediality and genre-bending strangeness of the work may also explain why it inspired a contemporary ballet. The director and choreographer Wayne McGregor collaborated with the artist Olafur Eliasson and composer Jamie xx to create *Tree of Codes* (2015), a ballet for the Manchester International Festival; McGregor calls the ballet "a translation" from "a book that has a body" into an art form composed of human bodies. See Studio Wayne McGregor, "*Tree of Codes* rehearsals, June 2015," 3:07, http://waynemcgregor.com/productions/tree-of-codes.

28. In his 1820–1821 play *Almansor*, Heine wrote, "Dort, wo man Bücher verbrennt, verbrennt man am Ende auch Menschen [Where they burn books, they will also ultimately burn people]."

29. Johanna Drucker, *The Century of Artists' Books* (New York: Granary, 1995).

30. https://briandettmer.com/.

31. "It was only under the pressure of the computer in the late 1980s that a new breed, the biblioclast, began to implement and execute their courteous affront." Allan Chasanoff, "Books, Codex, Bound," in *Doug Beube Breaking the Codex: Bookwork, Collage, and Mixed Media*, ed. Marian Cohn (Brooklyn: Etc. Etc. The Iconoclastic Museum Press, 2011), 13.

32. For an introduction to the artistic genre, see *Art Made from Books: Altered, Sculpted, Carved, Transformed*, comp. Laura Heyenga, pref. Brian Dettmer, intro. Alyson Kuhn (San Francisco: Chronicle, 2013).

33. Garrett Stewart, *Bookwork: Medium to Object to Concept to Art* (Chicago: University of Chicago Press, 2011), xiv, xiii.

34. Karen Ann Myers, "Curatorial Statement," in *Rebound: Dissections and Excavations in Book Art*, exhibition catalog (Charleston, SC: Halsey Institute of Contemporary Art, 2013), n.p.

35. For images and description, see *Doug Beube Breaking the Codex*, 26.

36. In *Doug Beube Breaking the Codex*, 172.

37. In *Doug Beube Breaking the Codex*, 67.

38. Qtd. in Jessica Pressman, "Bookwork and Bookishness: An Interview with Doug Beube and Brian Dettmer," in *Book Presence in a Digital Age*, ed. Kiene Brillenburg Wurth, Kari Driscoll, and Jessica Pressman (New York: Bloomsbury, 2018), 64.

39. Safran Foer, "This Book and The Book," 138.

40. See Harold Bloom, *The Anxiety of Influence: A Theory of Poetry* (New York: Oxford University Press, 1973).

41. Quoted in Heller, n.p.

42. Safran Foer, "This Book and The Book," 138.

43. Rebecca L. Walkowitz, *Born Translated: The Contemporary Novel in an Age of World Literature* (New York: Columbia University Press, 2015), 233. "Nowhere in the text or paratext . . . does the name of the translator or the language of composition appear. So, while Foer's project may emphasize the production, materiality, and history of 'the book' in some substantial ways, it occludes the production, materiality, and history of the book in translation" (232–33).

44. Safran Foer, "This Book and The Book," 137.

45. Emily Apter, introduction to *Fetishism as Cultural Discourse*, ed. Emily Apter and William Pietz (Ithaca, NY: Cornell University Press, 1993), 4.

46. For an extended discussion of the fetish and its etymology and purpose in bookishness, see chapter 3.

47. *Tree of Codes* was marketed as an artist book and become a fetishized object; its small initial print run ensured the latter. Specific numbers are not forthcoming, but the publisher's website does note that 30,000 copies were sold. Its digital production method should enable the book to be easily reprinted, but the publisher's strategy ensured that a book originally priced at $40 is now going for upward of $150. Thanks to David Kamper for helping me see this point. In point of fact, Safran Foer was able to make *Tree of Codes*, at least in part, because of who he is: a writer with proven market success. Alexander Starre describes *Tree of Codes* as "a prestige project corresponding to the trajectory of Foer's career" in *Metamedia: American Book Fictions and Literary Print Culture After Digitization* (Ames: University of Iowa Press, 2015), 244.

48. S. D. Chrostowska writes of "the centrality of the foot" and "the decidedly *pedicentric* universe of Schulz's drawings, etchings, and sketches" wherein women's feet, pointed and powerful in heels, appear throughout, but particularly in *The Booke of Idolatry*, which Chrostowska describes as "profusely depict[ing] masochistic scenes." S. D. Chrostowska, " 'Masochistic Art of Fantasy': The Literary Works

of Bruno Schulz in the Context of Modern Masochism," *Russian Literature* 55, no. 4 (2004): 477, 474. See also Rolando Perez, *The Divine Duty of Servants: A Book of Worship (Based on the Artwork of Bruno Schulz)* (Brooklyn: Cool Grove, 1999); and Taylor, "Childhood Revisited."

49. Schulz's story "The Book" appears in the collection *Sanatorium Under the Sign of the Hourglass* (1937).

50. Jerzy Ficowski, *Regions of the Great Heresy: Bruno Schulz, a Biographical Portrait*, trans. and ed. Theodosia Robertson (New York: Norton, 1992), 27. Ficowski dedicated his professional life to locating lost or hidden fragments of Schulz's work and to preserving the legacy of Bruno Schulz.

51. David A. Goldfarb, introduction to Bruno Schulz, *The Street of Crocodiles and Other Stories*, trans. Celina Wieniewska (New York: Penguin, 2008), xix.

CODA

1. Chris Colfer, *The Land of Stories: The Wishing Well* (New York: Little, Brown, 2012), 78–79.

2. Colfer, *The Land of Stories*, chapters 2, 3, 5. *The Land of Stories* is not the only bookishness series on my children's bookshelf. Consider also Mary Pope Osbourne's incredibly successful Magic Tree House series. The first installation, *Dinosaurs Before Dark*, was published in 1992, smack in the midst of brewing fears and laments about the death of the book due to digital technologies, and features another pair of siblings (Jack and Annie) using books as magic portals; their magic tree house contains books that help them travel back and forth in time.

3. "What makes children's literature possible is adult consciousness of childhood as a privileged time and space that's been lost, that's died, and that yet remains infinitely accessible to adult memory and imagination, through the medium of literature and the practices of literacy." Patricia Crain, *Reading Children: Literacy, Property, and the Dilemmas of Childhood in Nineteenth-Century America* (Philadelphia: University of Pennsylvania Press, 2016), 53. This helps explain (and historicize) my feelings while watching my daughter read.

4. Crain, *Reading Children*, 1.

5. The paper email notepad is not alone in expressing nostalgia for paper in the moment of web*pages*. There are Moleskin journals (that utmost bourgeois writing notebook) printed with the words "Press the Button to Start!" and artwork like that by the French artists Zim and Zou's *Back to Basics* (2011), a collection of handcrafted sculptures made from brightly colored paper that depicts old media devices, including a computer diskette.

6. Sara Ahmed, *The Cultural Politics of Emotion* (New York: Routledge, 2015), 90. "What sticks 'shows us' where the object has traveled through what it has gathered on its surface, gatherings that become a part of the object, and call into question its integrity as an object" (91).

7. As I was putting the finishing touches on the book you hold in your hands, Dan Cohen wrote an article for the *Atlantic* titled "The Books of College Libraries Are Turning Into Wallpaper" (May 26, 2019). He cites a 64 percent decline in the number of books checked out by undergraduates in the past decade but also notes that the decline in the use of books does not mean the students don't care about the books. "If books are becoming wallpaper, they *are* rather nice wallpaper, surrounding students with deep learning and with some helpful sound-deadening characteristics to boot," he quips, before asserting, "Beware the peril of books as glorified wallpaper." Wallpaper is the ultimate form of stickiness—it is sticky paper that transforms the walls of a room and, possibly, human interaction within it. Thanks to Rita Raley for bringing this article to my attention and for thinking through the book throughout its development.

INDEX

Aarseth, Espen, 178n7

Abrams, J. J., 23, 100. *See also* S.

Acland, Charles, 157n3

Ahmed, Sara, 156, 183n6

AI. *See* artificial intelligence

Amazon: convergence culture and, 18; as literary culture driving force, 18–19; market value, 18, 159n20

"American Scholar, The" (Emerson), 33

Anderson, Chris, 158n16

Anxiety of Obsolescence, The (Fitzpatrick), 57

Apple: iBooks, 35, *36*, 37–38; iPhone, *2*

Apter, Emily, 147

AR. *See* augmented reality

artificial intelligence (AI): Turing and, 87; writing and, 103, 107, 173n30

Artificial Kingdom, The (Olalquiaga), 172n17

attachment: digital culture and, 24; literary studies and, 20; methodology and, 20–21

Augé, Marc, 177n38

augmented reality (AR): *Between Page and Screen* and, 70–71, 72, 168n18; *The Ice-Bound Concordance* as, 103–4

Austen, Jane: commodities and, 158n7; duvet cover and, *11*, 11–13; fakery and, 92, *92*, *93*, 94–95

Back to Basics (Zim and Zou), 183n5

Barchas, Janine, 158n7

Baudrillard, Jean, 88

Benjamin, Walter, 86

Bernays, Edward, 89–90, 91

Between Page and Screen (Borsuk and Bouse), 22; anthropomorphized objects in, 71–72; AR and, 70–71, 72, 168n18; digital networks and, 69–70; *How the Page Matters*

Between Page and Screen (continued)
and, 169n22; as it-text, 69–72;
QR codes and, 70, *70*, 72,
168n18; reading as atypical in,
71; "Re-Orienting Ourselves
Towards the Material" and,
169n21
Beube, Doug, 151; bookworks of,
142–44, *144*; on his art, 144;
Inside Macintosh by, 143, *144*
Birkets, Sven, 27–28
blooks, 89, *90*, 171n8
Blooks (Dubanksy), *90*, 171n8
Böhme, Hartmut, 167n7
Bolter, Jay David, 88, 115
BookBook device cover, 2, *2*, 153
Booke of Idolatry, The (Schulz), 148,
181n48
"Bookishness in the Digital Age"
(symposium), 117–18
books: death of, 25–31, 160n5,
162n21; defined, 61; materiality
of, 1–2; novel equaling, 79; as
residual media, 8; symbolism
surrounding, 2–3. *See also
specific topics*
bookshelf, digital, 35, *36*, 37–38
"Books of College Libraries Are
Turning Into Wallpaper, The"
(Cohen), 183n7
bookwork: as book-based sculpture
genre, 8; demediation and, 8;
sculpture, 142–44, *144*; *Slash* and,
8, *9*, 10; *Tree of Codes* and, 140–48
Borsuk, Amaranth, 22. *See also
Between Page and Screen*

Boscagli, Maurizia, 83
Bouse, Brad, 22. *See also Between
Page and Screen*
Broch, Hermann, 95–96
Burton, Tim, 73, 169n30

Cakes and Cupcakes Mumbai, 6
Calinescu, Matei, 172n17
Carr, Nicolas, 27–28, 160n6
cell-phone cover, 2, *2*
Chasanoff, Allan, 180n31
children's literature: Crain and,
152–53, 182n3; *It's a Book*, 14;
Press Here, 14–15
Cinnamon Shops, 177n2
class: bookishness as about, 12;
books a symbols of, 56; kitsch
and, 96; shelter and, 56–59
codex: as sacred object, 61, 166nn1–2;
semiotics, 38; Stallybrass on,
166n1; wood and, 145
Cohen, Dan, 183n7
Colfer, Chris, 151–52
Comfort, Alex, 78
commodity fetishism, 79, 169n31
Complete Untitled Film Stills, The
(Sherman), 82–83
Conrad, Joseph, 68
convergence culture, 18, 159n19
Crain, Patricia: children's literature
and, 152–53, 182n3; codicology
of modern self and, 162n26; *The
Story of A* by, 165n16
Cramer, Florian, 135
culture: Amazon and, 18–19; *The
Anxiety of Obsolescence* and, 57;

convergence, 18, 159n19; discourse network and, 175n20; *Fetishism and Culture*, 167n7; hegemonic values and, 162n27; Murray on literary, 31; participatory, 159n19; playbor, 58, 166n28; residual and, 7; review, 172n15; shallow, 27–28. *See also* digital culture

cupcakes, 6

Cybertext (Aarseth), 178n7

Danielewski, Mark Z., 23, 41. *See also House of Leaves*

Debray, Régis, 165n19, 166n2

Delayed Response (Farman), 162n21

Dettmer, Brian, 8, *9*

Digital Contagions (Parikka), 176n36

digital culture: attachment and, 24; creative reactions to, 1–2; discourse network and, 175n20; fakery operating in, 22–23; fear surrounding, 17; *It's a Book* and, 14; *Press Here* and, 14–15; shelfies and, 35, 163n38; thereness of books and, 63; Y2K and, 17

digital reading devices: codex semiotics and, 38; history of, 15, 158n13; "With Kindle, Can You Tell It's Proust?," 34

Dinosaurs Before Dark (Osbourne), 182n2

discourse network, 175n20, 179n22

Domínguez, Carlos María, 22. *See also House of Paper, The*

Don Quixote (Cervantes), 33

Dorst, Doug, 23. *See also S.*

Dubanksy, Mindell, 89, 171n8

dummy spine, 89–90, 171n7

duvet cover, *11*, 11–13

Dworkin, Craig, 19–20

Egan, Jennifer, 21. *See also Keep, The; Visit from the Goon Squad, A*

Eisenstein, Elizabeth, 26

Elias, Norbert, 95

Emerson, Ralph Waldo, 33

Erasmus, 26

e-reader. *See* digital reading devices

ergodic, 178n7

Execution of Mary, Queen of Scots, The (stop-motion film), 77

Extremely Loud & Incredibly Close (Foer), 21; bookish allegory of, 49–51; conclusions about, 50–51; paperless world and, 49–50; reconstitution and, 48–51; as scrapbook and archive, 49; *The Zero* compared with, 48–49

Faber, Michel, 179n26

Faces of Modernity (Calinescu), 172n17

Fadiman, Anne, 62

fakery: Austen, 92, *92*, *93*, 94–95; binary oppositions and, 88–89; blooks and, 89, *90*, 171n8; computing and, 87; connection fostered via, 86; contemporary literature and, 96–103; digital culture operating via, 22–23; digital interfaces and, 88; digital

fakery (*continued*)
    reproduction and, 86; dummy
    spine, 89–90, 171n7; *The
    Ice-Bound Concordance* as, 103–8,
    104, 106; kitsch, 92–103; literary
    criticism and, 171n7; literary
    forgeries, 89, 171n7; metaphor
    and, 88; overview, 86; perfume
    and, 85–86; remediation and, 88;
    S. as, 96–103, *98, 99*; second-degree
    nature of, 94–95; Siri and, 87;
    support systems and, 91–92;
    Target.com stack of books,
    90–91, *91*; Turing and, 86–87
*Fantastic Flying Books of Mr. Morris
    Lessmore, The* (Joyce), 21;
    bookishness of, 52; conclusions
    about, 52–53; reconnection and,
    51–53
Farman, Jason, 162n21
Feast (Beube), 143
Felski, Rita, 20
fetish: commodity fetishism, 79,
    169n31; Freud and, 167n9;
    history surrounding, 63–64,
    167n7; *The Joy of Books* and,
    73–79; materiality and, 64;
    memorial and, 147–48; objects
    and souvenirs, 73–84; Pietz and,
    64, 167n7; Schulz and, 147–48,
    181n48; stop-motion film and,
    77; *Tree of Codes* and, 147–48,
    181n47
Fetishism and Culture (Böhme),
    167n7
Ficowski, Jerzy, 148, 182n50

Fiore, Quentin, 19
Fitzgerald, F. Scott, 33
Fitzpatrick, Kathleen, 57
Foer, Jonathan Safran, 21, 23–24;
    creative process of, 134–35;
    lies of, 145–46; memorial and,
    130–31; Schulz and, 134, 145;
    Western Wall and, 147;
    Wieniewska on, 146, 181n43.
    See also Tree of Codes
Foucault, Michel, 162n22
Freud, Sigmund: fetish and,
    167n9; mystic writing pad
    and, 163n31

Garbe, Jacob, 23. *See also Ice-Bound
    Concordance, The*
Gioia, Dana, 29
Gitelman, Lisa, 29
Going West (stop-motion film), 75–76
Gravity's Rainbow (Pynchon), 139
Great Gatsby, The (Fitzgerald), 33
Grusin, Richard, 88, 115
Gutenberg Elegies, The (Birkets),
    27–28
Gutenberg Galaxy, The (McLuhan), 48

Hall, Steven, 23. *See also Raw Shark
    Texts, The*
handwriting, digitally printed,
    101–2
Haunted (Poe), 113, 114, 174n9
Hayles, N. Katherine: binary code
    and, 137, 179n17; on digitality,
    18; digital production processes
    and, 178n10; on information

and body separation, 119; *Tree of Codes* and, 179n25

headboard, *3*

Heidegger, Martin, 178n6

Heine, Heinrich, 141, 180n28

Hesse, Carla, 58

Holocaust, 24, 141, 147

Home (Lagos), 120

House of Leaves (Danielewski), 23, 41, 168n19; bookbound literature and, 117; conclusions about, 127–28; digital environment and, 115; digital manipulation spectre in, 116; fears exploited in, 115; as foundation for bookishness, 110–11; house in, 111, 116–17; multimedia network of, 113–15, 174n9; as networked novel, 112–13, 174n9; overview about, 109–11; page design in, 112, *113*; *S.* compared with, 100; shelter and, 41–42, 115–16; as weapon, 110–17

House of Paper, The (Domínguez), 22; book as thing and, 67–69; book-object in, 67–68; books as bricks in, 69; magical realism and, 67

How the Page Matters (Mak), 169n22

How to Do Things with Books in Victorian England (Price), 28

Hudson, Nicolas, 65

Hugo, Victor, 25

Huhtamo, Erkki, 160n5

Humpty Dumpty Circus, The (stop-motion film), 77

Humument, A (Phillips), 142

Hunchback of Notre Dame, The (Hugo), 25

Hungerford, Amy, 172n24

iBooks, 35, *36*, 37–38

Ice-Bound Concordance, The (Reed and Garbe), 23; anthropocentric assumptions related to, 105, 107; as AR literature, 103–4; author-figure and, 107; conclusions, 107–8; first narrative in, 103–4; as kitsch, 103–8, *104*, *106*; scrapbook in, 105, *106*; second narrative in, 104–5

identification: bookishness and, 10; constructing and projecting, 12; selfhood and, 32, 33–34

Important Artifacts and Personal Property from the Collection of Lenore Doolan and Harold Morris, Including Books, Street Fashion, and Jewelry (Shapton), 22; books depicted in, 82; *The Complete Untitled Film Stills* in, 82–83; formatting of objects in, 83; narrative style of, 80; opening of, 80–82; page layout from, *81*; souvenir and, 80–84; as stuff catalog, 83–84

Inside Macintosh (Beube), 143, *144*

Interfaith (Beube), 143

"Is Google Making Us Stupid?" (Carr), 27–28, 160n6

-ishness, 10

it-narrative: eighteenth century, 65; nineteenth century, 65–66

It's a Book (Smith), 14

it-text: *Between Page and Screen*, 69–72; book as thing and, 64–67; *The House of Paper*, 67–69; it-narrative and, 65–66; networked perspective and, 66–67; object-oriented perspective of, 66, 168n12

Jenkins, Henry, 20, 159n19

Johnson, Steven, 88

Jonze, Spike, 76

Joyce, William, 21. *See also Fantastic Flying Books of Mr. Morris Lessmore, The*

Joy of Books, The (Ohlenkamps), 22; ending scene in, 74, *75*; independent bookstores and, 78–79; opening scene in, 73; screenshot, *75*; social media and, 78; stop-motion bookishness and, 73–79; success of, 73–74; YouTube and, 78, 170n32

Joy of Sex, The, 77–78

Keep, The (Egan), 21; books and digital life interwoven in, 44–45; immersion and, 45–46; literature as refuge and, 44; narratives in, 43–44; refuge and, 43–46; style of, 43

Kindle: history of, 15, 158n13; "With Kindle, Can You Tell It's Proust?," 34

Kirschenbaum, Matthew, 30, 177n37

kitsch: Broch and, 95–96; class and, 96; comforter as, 92, *92*; connection and, 96; contemporary literature and, 96–103; defined, 95; eighteenth-century and, 172n19; fakery and, 92–103; humor and, 92, *92, 93*, 94; *The Ice-Bound Concordance* as, 103–8, *104, 106*; leggings, 92, *92, 93*, 94–95; modernity and, 172n17; S. as, 96–103, *98, 99*

Kittler, Friedrich, 175n20, 179n22

Land of Stories, The (Colfer), 151–52

leggings, 92, *92, 93*, 94–95

Le-Tan, Olympia, 76

Library (Ullman), 141

"Literacy Debate" (*New York Times*), 15–17

Liu, Alan, 119, 175n20, 176n34

Locke, John, 163n31

Los Angeles International Airport store, 3, 6

Loving Literature (Lynch), 21

Lupton, Christina, 58

Lynch, Deidre Shauna: on assumptions about reading, 28; *Loving Literature* by, 21

Mac BookBook (Twelve South), 6–7, *7*

Mak, Bonnie: character of book owner and, 33–34; *How the Page Matters* by, 169n22

Making Literature Now (Hungerford), 172n24

"Making *Tree of Codes*" (Visual
Editions), 134
Mauro, Aaron, 178n8, 179n19
McFadden, Dave, 7. *See also Slash*
exhibit
McGann, Jerome, 133
McGregor, Wayne, 180n27
McGurl, Mark, 18
McLuhan, Marshall: on collide-
oscope of interfaced situations,
19; global village and, 124,
175n29; *The Zero* and, 48
Medium Is the Massage, The
(McLuhan and Fiore), 19
memorial function: fetish and,
147–48; Foer and, 130–31; *Library*
and, 141; overview, 23–24;
sculpture, bookwork, and,
142–44, *144*; *Tree of Codes*, 129–48
Mitchell, William J., 116
Moleskin journals, 183n5
Montemagno, Buonaccorso da,
33–34
*Mourir auprès de toi. See To Die by
Your Side*
Mr. Penumbra's 24-Hour Bookstore
(Sloan), 21–22; book as sacred
and, 53–54, 165n19; digitality
and, 55–56; medium is message
in, 54–55; recognition and,
53–56
Murphy, Priscilla Coit, 160n5
Murray, Simone: on literary
culture, 31; on review culture,
172n15
My Silver Planet (Tiffany), 172n19

Nabokov, Vladimir, 100
National Endowment for the Arts
(NEA), 29–30
necklace, 4
network: digital, 69–70; discourse,
175n20, 179n22; geographically
distributed, 134, 178n8; *House of
Leaves* and, 112–15, 174n9;
it-text and, 66–67
New Funk Standards (Dettmer), 8, *9*
New Orleans store window, 5
New York Times: "Literacy Debate"
in, 15–17; "With Kindle, Can You
Tell It's Proust?," 34
Ngai, Sianne, 100–101
Non-Places (Augé), 177n38
novel: AI assistance in writing, 107,
173n30; book equaling, 79;
it-narrative and, 65; *The Raw
Shark Texts* and, 126–27;
technology and, 57. *See also
specific works*
Nunberg, Geoffrey, 29–30

Occhipinti, Lisa, 13
Ohlenkamp, Lisa, 22, 169n23
Ohlenkamp, Sean, 22, 169n23,
170n33
Olalquiaga, Celeste, 172n17
Organizing the Bookcase (Ohlenkamp
and Ohlenkamp), 169n23
Osbourne, Mary Pope, 182n2

Pale Fire (Nabokov), 100
Paper E-mail (notepad), 153–56, *154*
Paper perfume, 85–86

Parikka, Jussi, 176n36

participatory culture, 159n19

Paulsrud, Pamela, 8, *9*

Petroski, Henry, 37

Phillips, Tom, 142

Pietz, William, 64, 167n7

Piper, Andrew, 21; on looking at books, 52–53; thereness of books and, 38–39, 63

playbor culture, 58, 166n28

Poe (recording artist), 113, 114, 174n9

power: books a symbols of, 56; colonization and, 32–33; of objects, 155–56

Press Here (Tullet), 14–15

Price, Leah, 20–21; on death of books, 26; *How to Do Things with Books in Victorian England* by, 28; "The Subconscious Shelf" by, 171n7; *What We Talk About When We Talk About Books* by, 162n21

Pride and Prejudice (Austen): comforter, 92, *92*; duvet cover, *11*, 11–13; leggings, 92, *92*, *93*, 94–95

"Problem of the Fetish, The" (Pietz), 167n7

prosumption, 159n19

punch-hole programming, 131, *132*

Pynchon, Thomas, 139

QR. *See* quick response codes

"Question Concerning Technology, The" (Heidegger), 178n6

quick response codes (QR), 70, *70*, 72, 168n18

Raw Shark Texts, The (Hall), 23; "Bookishness in the Digital Age" and, 117–18; books as shelter in, 120–21; conclusions about, 127–28; concrete-poetry shark in, *122*; disembodied digital information and, 118–19; disembodied posthuman monster in, 125–26; fiction and, 126–27; flip-book sequence in, 121, *123*; ignorance of digital technology and, 124, 176n30; Ludovician shark in, 119–20, 121, 124, 127; message and medium related to, 118–19, 175n20; opening of, 119; overview about, 109–10; Rorschach test and, 127; un-space and, 126, 177n38; as weapon, 117–28

reading: *Between Page and Screen* and, 71; Birkets and Carr perspectives on, 27–28; book repurposing and, 13; close, 155; cover-to-cover, 28–29, 161n14; innocence in, 149–50; "Literacy Debate" and, 15–17; Lynch on, 28; shallow, 27–28; Stallybrass and, 29, 161n13; *Tree of Codes*, 131–48. *See also* digital reading devices

"Reading at Risk" (NEA), 29–30

Reed, Aaron A., 23. *See also* *Ice-Bound Concordance, The*

Reichelt, Victoria, 163n38

Remediation (Bolter and Grusin), 88

Repurposed Library, The (Occhipinti), 13

residual media, 7

Residual Media (Acland), 157n3

Rorschach test, 127

S. (Abrams and Dorst), 23; characters of, 97; conclusions about, 102–3, 107–8; digitally printed handwriting in, 101–2; fakery and, 96–103, *98, 99*; interested judgment and, 100–101; as knockoff, 100; marginalia in, *99*; Ngai and, 100–101; novel-within-a-novel, 97, 99–100; physical presence and, 101, 172n24; real versus fake and, 100; slipcove and insert elements from, 97, *98*; Theseus's Paradox and, 99–100; works compared with, 100

Scholz, Trebor, 166n28

Schulz, Bruno: fetish of, 147–48, 181n48; Ficowski and, 148, 182n50; Foer and, 134, 145; Wieniewska on, 146. *See also Booke of Idolatry, The*; *Street of Crocodiles, The*

sculpture, bookwork, 8, 142–44, *144*

"Sense, Sensibility, and Soap" (Barchas), 158n7

Sexuality and the Psychology of Love (Freud), 167n9

Shadow-Line, The (Conrad), 68

Shapton, Leanne, 22. *See also Important Artifacts and Personal Property from the Collection of Lenore Doolan and Harold Morris, Including Books, Street Fashion, and Jewelry*

shelfies, 35, 163n38

Sherman, Cindy, 82–83

simulacra, of Baudrillard, 7, 88, 157n1

Siri, 87

Slash exhibit: bookwork and, 8, 9, 10; overview about, 7–8; paper and, 7–10

Sloane, Robin, 21–22, 173n30. *See also Mr. Penumbra's 24-Hour Bookstore*

slow movements, 58, 166n29

Smith, Lane, 14

social media: connection and, 150–51; history, 15; *The Joy of Books* and, 78; nearness to books via, 12; shelfies and, 35

"Some Non-Textual Uses of Books" (Watson), 171n7

souvenirs: *Important Artifacts and Personal Property from the Collection of Lenore Doolan and Harold Morris, Including Books, Street Fashion, and Jewelry* and, 80–84; longing and, 84; objects and, 73–84

Stallybrass, Peter: on codex, 166n1; scroll versus book and, 29, 161n13

Starre, Alexander, 181n47

Stevens, Kati, 91

Stewart, Garrett, 8, 142, 163n38

stickiness, from Ahmed, 156, 183nn6–7

stop-motion film: *The Execution of Mary, Queen of Scots*, 77; fetish and, 77; *Going West*, 75–76; *The Humpty Dumpty Circus*, 77; *The Joy of Books*, 73–79; *Organizing the Bookcase*, 169n23; renaissance in, 77–78; *This Is Where We Live*, 76; *To Die by Your Side*, 76

Story of A, The (Crain), 165n16

Street of Crocodiles, The (Schulz): Cinnamon Shops and, 177n2; fetish and, 147; Foer and, 134, 145; "This Book and The Book" referencing, 147; *Tree of Codes* and, 129–30

"Subconscious Shelf, The" (Price), 171n7

Tanderup, Sara, 52

Target.com stack of books, 90–91, *91*

terrorism, 41, 46

textual condition, McGann, 18, 158n18

Theseus's Paradox, 99–100

thing, book as: codex and, 61, 166nn1–2; conclusions, 84; examples of, 61; fetish objects and, 73–84; *The House of Paper* and, 67–69; it-narrative and, 65–66; it-texts and, 64–67; *The Joy of Books* and, 73–79; meaning and, 62; overview, 22, 64; physical presence and, 62–63

"This Book and The Book" (Foer), 146–47

This Is Where We Live (stop-motion film), 76

Thorburn, David, 20

Tiffany, Daniel, 172n19

To Die by Your Side (stop-motion film), 76

Touchstones (Paulsrud), 8, *9*

Track Changes (Kirschenbaum), 177n37

Tree of Codes (Foer): ballet inspired by, 180n27; beginning of, 136; comet and, 139–40; conclusions about, 135, 140, 144, 148; cover design, 131, *132*, 133; creative process used in, 134–35; criticism of, 140–41, 179nn25–26; end of, 139–40; father and, 140; fetish and, 147–48, 181n47; fragmented narrative of, 135–36; generational shift and, 137; genre hybridity of, 140, 180n27; geographically distributed network producing, 134, 178n8; Hayles and, 179n25; as Holocaust literature, 141; *A Humument* compared with, 142; interaction and, 133–34, 178n7; "Making *Tree of Codes*," 134; marketing of, 181n47; medialities utilized in, 133, 177n3; memorial function, 129–48; memorial to her in, 138–39; overview, 23–24; page layout of, 129–30, *130*; page turning in, 133–34, 146, 178n6; as post-digital object, 135; preprint textuality and, 138;

presence and absence and, 137–38; reading, 131–48; reading afterword of, 145–48; reading bookwork in, 140–48; reading of text, 135–40; sculpture, bookwork, and, 142; *The Street of Crocodiles* and, 129–30, 145; "This Book and The Book" in, 146–47; transcribing content of pages of, 135–36, 178n13; verso side of pages in, 134; Visual Editions and, 131, 134; whisper metaphor related to, 179n19; Wieniewska and, 146, 181n43; word separation and, 138; writing-as-cutting process in, 130; Wurth on, 177n3

Tullet, Hervé, 14–15

Turing, Alan, 86–87

Twin Towers (Beube), 143

Ullman, Micha, 141

Vaidhyanathan, Siva, 54

"Versioning Loss" (Mauro), 178n8, 179n19

vinyl records, 163n30

Visit from the Goon Squad, A (Egan), 43

Visual Editions, 131, 134

wallpaper, 183n7

Walter, Jess, 21. *See also Zero, The*

Watson, Rowan, 171n7

weapon, book as: *House of Leaves*, 110–17; overview, 23; *The Raw Shark Texts*, 117–28

"Web Is Dead, Long Live the Internet, The " (Anderson and Wolff), 158n16

Western Wall, 147

What We Talk About When We Talk About Books (Price), 162n21

Wieniewska, Celina, 146, 181n43

Williams, Raymond, 7, 157n3

"With Kindle, Can You Tell It's Proust?" (*New York Times*), 34

Wolff, Michael, 158n16

writing: AI and, 103, 107, 173n30; digitally printed handwriting, 101–2; mystic writing pad, 163n31; writing-as-cutting process, 130

Wurth, Kiene Brillenburg, 177n3, 179n25

Y2K, 17

YouTube, 78, 170n32

Zero, The (Walter), 21; conclusions about, 50–51; Documentation department in, 47–48; *Extremely Loud & Incredibly Close* compared with, 48–49; McLuhan and, 48; paper permeating, 46–48; reconstitution and, 46–48; terrorism and, 46

Zim and Zou, 183n5

LITERATURE NOW

MATTHEW HART, DAVID JAMES, AND
REBECCA L. WALKOWITZ, SERIES EDITORS

Caren Irr, *Toward the Geopolitical Novel: U.S. Fiction in the
Twenty-First Century*

Heather Houser, *Ecosickness in Contemporary U.S. Fiction:
Environment and Affect*

Mrinalini Chakravorty, *In Stereotype: South Asia in
the Global Literary Imaginary*

Héctor Hoyos, *Beyond Bolaño: The Global Latin American Novel*

Rebecca L. Walkowitz, *Born Translated: The Contemporary Novel
in an Age of World Literature*

Carol Jacobs, *Sebald's Vision*

Sarah Phillips Casteel, *Calypso Jews: Jewishness in the
Caribbean Literary Imagination*

Jeremy Rosen, *Minor Characters Have Their Day: Genre and
the Contemporary Literary Marketplace*

Jesse Matz, *Lasting Impressions: The Legacies of Impressionism
in Contemporary Culture*

Ashley T. Shelden, *Unmaking Love: The Contemporary Novel and
the Impossibility of Union*

Theodore Martin, *Contemporary Drift: Genre, Historicism, and
the Problem of the Present*

Zara Dinnen, *The Digital Banal: New Media and American
Literature and Culture*

Gloria Fisk, *Orhan Pamuk and the Good of World Literature*

Peter Morey, *Islamophobia and the Novel*

Sarah Chihaya, Merve Emre, Katherine Hill, and Jill Richards,
The Ferrante Letters: An Experiment in Collective Criticism

Christy Wampole, *Degenerative Realism: Novel and
Nation in Twenty-First-Century France*

Heather Houser, *Infowhelm: Environmental Art and
Literature in an Age of Data*